Praise for Birdie Jaworski

Her posts draw more than 1,000 hits a day from readers fascinated by the woman who buys antiwrinkle cream for her pet monkey Hubert or by the wife who orders Bust-Sculpt Contouring ointment for her husband, who ingests it as an alternative to Viagra.
- *Time Magazine*

What Birdie discovered about people – and herself – went more than skin deep.
- *Positive Thinking Magazine*

Birdie Jaworski, an Avon Products Inc. representative in rural Las Vegas, N.M., has developed one of the most popular blogs hosted at news web site Salon.com ... One reason for Ms. Jaworski's popularity: her unvarnished reviews of Avon products, which she tries before peddling to customers.

- *Wall Street Journal*

Copyright 2011
Gallinas Girls Publishing
All Rights Reserved

100 Ways to Sell AVON

by Birdie Jaworski

Gallinas Girls Publishing
Las Vegas, New Mexico

This book is dedicated to every Avon Lady who still seeks new friends, new money for her pocket, new memories by knocking on strange doors. I still sell Avon, and my heart knows your joys, your struggle.

Much love from Birdie

~ ~ ~

Also by Birdie Jaworski

Don't Shoot! I'm Just the Avon Lady

My Tiny Vegas

GALLINAS: Sixteen Months with a Biweekly Magazine Featuring the Arts, Cultures and Communities of Northeastern New Mexico

And look for *100 Ways to Recruit* coming soon!

Table of Contents

Introduction	1-4
Ways 1-20	5-24
Story Time	
Balls to the Wall	25-29
Not-Quite-A-Prank-Call, Part One	29-30
Ways 21-40	31-50
Tips of the Trade	
Brochures	51
Business Card Experiment	52
Beauty Tip Cards	53
Make the Most of your eRep Site	54
Be an Environmentally Friendly Avon Rep	55-56
Ways 41-60	57-76
Story Time	
Jesucristo	77-81
Sample Fundraising Letter	82
Ways 61-80	83-102
Product Reviews: Know your Avon	103-108
Story Time	
I Animal Test an Avon Product	109-110
11 Guerrilla Marketing Avon Techniques	111-113
Not-Quite-A-Prank-Call, Part Two	113-114
Ways 81-100	115-134
104 Uses of Skin So Soft	135-140

Introduction

Avon Lady Evangelist

My Avon district sales manager sat next to me at my kitchen table a few years ago. She wore soft caramel lipstick to match her Asian print jacket, a shade just two tones shy of her sculpted bouffant.

"Birdie," she said, her index pointing first to her lips, then mine, "every woman buys lipstick. Your new Avon business manual shows you how to sell the exact type of lipstick your customer needs. Here, take a look."

I glanced at the open blue binder, at a chart where you can match up hydration versus long-wearing versus affordability, ingredients, lifestyle, you name it. Each of the core Avon lipsticks was dissected, outlined, splayed on the page like an alien anatomy diagram. I nodded my head as if I beheld the sacred Tibetan Book of the Dead. I made a mental note to memorize these facts FIRST!

Some years later, I can still cite the Lipstick Mantras, spill them into the palm of a questioning customer. I deliver Avon brochures along the short streets of my small town. I sell lipsticks and deodorant door-to-door, canvass an area of a couple hundred homes hidden by juniper and cedar, a place still untouched by the recent years of rocket-crazy real estate investors. I leave my books on faded wooden door steps and cracked driveways. I wait for customers to call with orders. I demonstrate delicate lotions and spray perfumes.

Most of the time it's a tough business. I feel the hurricane burst of slamming doors. I track down customers with bad checks. Sometimes Avon does me wrong, sends me the wrong product, charges me the wrong amount. Sometimes my boys miss school with the flu and I can't toss my mascara to the wind. Sometimes good things happen - I meet a rich customer with an open wallet, I make a new friend, I find a product I love.

If the mystics are right, and you choose your own obstacles through many lifetimes, I picked my road this time around to be hidden and lumpy and snaking through dark sticky brambles, full of brochures left in doctor's waiting rooms and stacked in neat piles next to DEET-enhanced bug sprays at wind torn campground stores. And all the while my heart sings songs about the way I was, the way I am, the way I might someday be, maybe a rich Avon Lady touring Thailand, or a broke Avon Lady eating peanut butter, maybe somebody between, maybe someone quite different.

I didn't start out an evangelist. It crept up on me. I just wanted to make a few bucks, buy my boys ice cream, pay the electric, the water, the mortgage. I wanted to get over my fear of knocking on strange doors. I wanted to keep a diary of my experiences, maybe pick up an internet customer or two. I set up a blog. I started writing, posting street and customer and bubble bath like some kind of trailer park diner menu. I didn't expect anyone to listen. I didn't expect to like Avon.

But something strange happened, something I didn't expect. I started experimenting with my Avon goodies and discovered I liked a lot of them! Not all of them, mind you, but enough to keep me interested, keep me telling potential customers and my two blog readers that I kinda liked Avon. Avon is OK, I posted. I tested a few more items. I wrote truthful reviews - some of them positive, some of them bad. More visitors came to sit at my blog, wait for another piece of my puzzle. I knocked on more doors. I sold more product. I met people with pasts, with character, with bushy eyebrows and a million pet cats. I told their stories, told about my Avon connection to them.

Selling Avon gave me determination and a reason to open my mouth, and the wider I opened, the more flies I captured, the more wings and legs I spit on the digital page. I became a spider with a web, but I let my prey go, let them read my stories and reviews and make decisions for themselves. I expected a hand slap from Avon HQ, expected my independent rep pink slip and a letter explaining how I was doing Avon wrong. It never came. We love you, District Managers wrote. We love your stories, the Avon call center employees posted.

Years later I field a few hundred inquiries a week. Tell me about Avon, they ask, tell me about the products, tell me whether I should sell it, too.

Yeah, I tell them, every one of them. Give it a try.

Avon gave me a reason to connect to humanity, a reason to extend my hand to touch another person. Avon gave me a backpack of glamour, and though my skin glows pink and my legs are soft and smooth, the real beauty happens every time I knock on a door and a new person answers.

I reached the level of Honor Society by using the tips and techniques in this book. Selling Avon is as easy as getting your brochure into the right hands. For new Avon Reps - and for experiences ones as well - that can be a tough order to fill! Meeting people is scary and full of uncertainty, but using these easy ideas, you will meet so many people in creative ways that you will find your order book filled. The tips in this book won't make you feel stressed or nervous - they are fun, easy to follow, and allow you to choose the level of contact with your potential customer that is most comfortable for you.

Have fun putting these tips into practice! I recommend just browsing through the book and choosing ideas that sound fun to you.

Mark the book with your own thoughts on each tip, and take notes on what worked out in the field. Selling Avon isn't a regular sort of sales job. Selling Avon is a way to share beauty, life, and stories with customers, many of whom will turn out to be great friends.

This book will help YOU grow your own Avon business, will help you find your own connections to new customers, new friends. Enjoy.

Avon in their Inbox!

1. Are you collecting your customers' email addresses? You should be! Start an e-newsletter at Constant Contact or Mail Chimp and send out a Campaign Blast every two weeks with the latest and greatest in the most recent Avon brochure. Add customer testimonials, photos of Befores and Afters, and lists of ways that Avon can help your customers achieve soft, supple skin or the perfect party look. Make sure you ask your customer if she would like to be added to your special list. Offer a thank you lip balm, sample, or nail file.

Sample First Campaign Blast Title: Beauty in Your Inbox! Avon Tips, Tricks, and Specials for YOU!

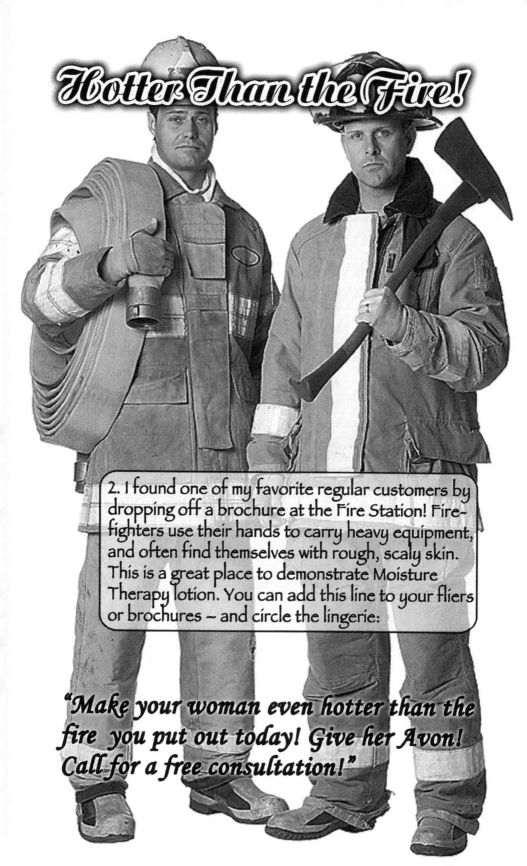

Make a Splash With Avon!

3. City pool in the summer, and indoor pools in the winter are the perfect locations to leave sunscreen and body care samples! Write on the cover of your Avon brochure:

"Avon is a Lifesaver!"

May is for Mascara!

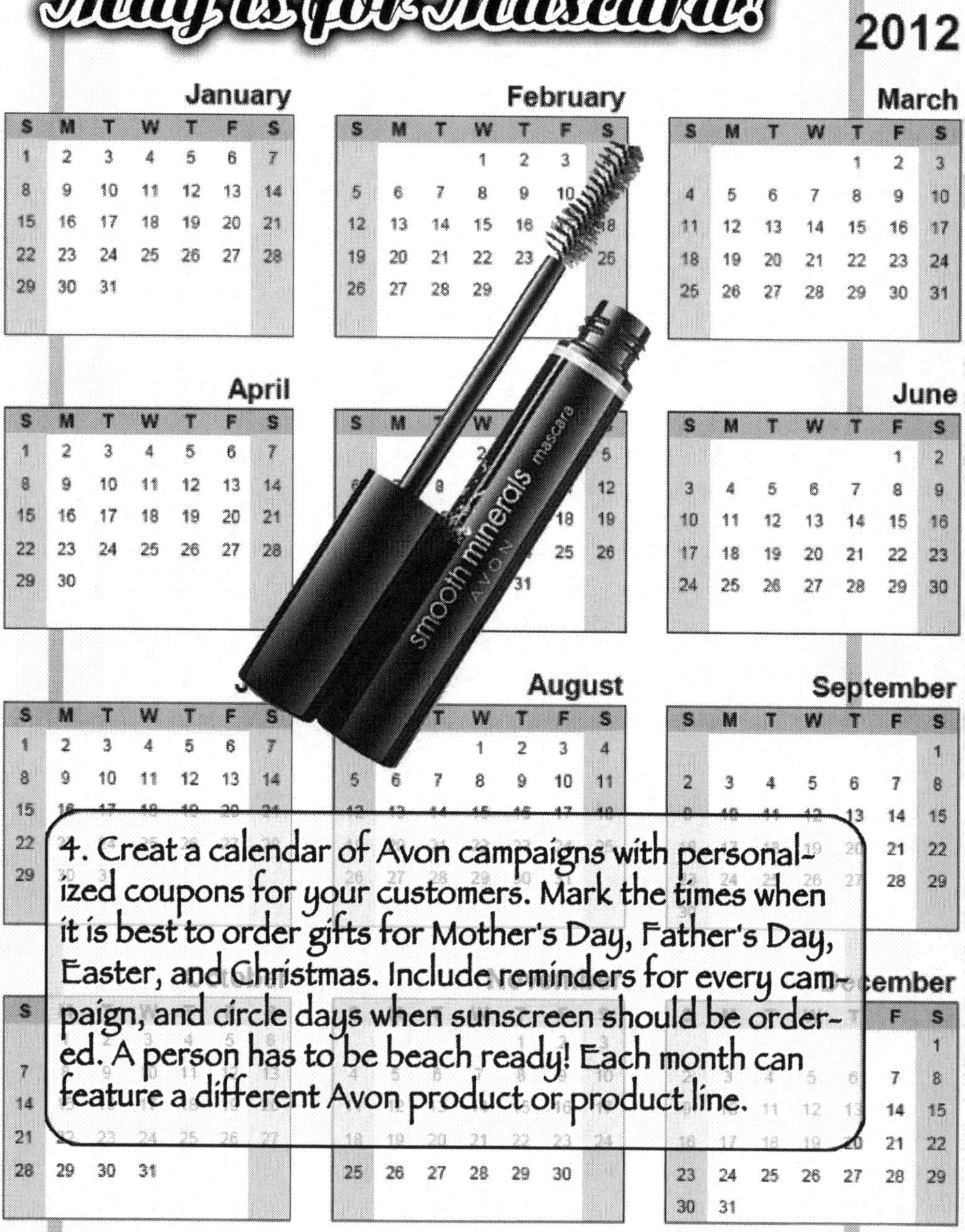
2012
January
February
March
April
June
August
September
smooth minerals mascara
AVON

4. Creat a calendar of Avon campaigns with personalized coupons for your customers. Mark the times when it is best to order gifts for Mother's Day, Father's Day, Easter, and Christmas. Include reminders for every campaign, and circle days when sunscreen should be ordered. A person has to be beach ready! Each month can feature a different Avon product or product line.

September is Skin Care Month!

Drop where they Shop!

5. The mall has an endless amount of places where you can leave your sales literature – the food court, dressing rooms, restrooms, the information kiosk. Some malls have a special rack for brochures or a bulletin board where you can post a flier. Write on your brochures:

"*Let me bring the beauty mall to you*"

Perfected!

6. Senior citizen centers are full of women and men who could use a little pampering and care in their life. Bring lots of free samples and brochures, and ask the receptionist if you can leave a stack at her desk for caregivers. You can add a stickie note to the front of your fliers that says:

"Avon: Since 1886. Not old. Perfected."

Hard Working Hands

7. Don't laugh, but plumbers, garbage collectors, and electricians make GREAT Avon customers! When you need your home serviced, prepare a special package for your workman or woman. Include a demo tube of Moisture Therapy hand cream, samples of fragrances, and a complimentary lip balm. It's hard working with your hands all day, and a little pampering feels so good.

"Don't let rough hands throw a wrench in the works!"

Link In!

8. Connect with other professionals using LinkedIn.com, a site for those who want to network with others. Let your contacts know that you are serious about your Avon business. This is a great way to get the word out that you are able to sell anyone - anywhere - Avon. Post your office hours, link to your Twitter & Facebook account, and upload your email address book so that you can find friends, business associates, and family members who would like to be connected online.

Your Avon business is only as serious as YOU are.

B & B and B:
Bed & Breakfast and Beauty!

9. Bring plenty of samples and a few brochures to any Bed and Breakfast establishment in your area. Tell the proprietors that you can furnish them with samples for their guests if they place regular orders.

"Wake up to Avon!"

AVON!

11. Attending a PTO meeting? A sing-a-long? A convention of Basset Hound Lovers? Decorate your name tag with the AVON logo! Let every other attendee know that you not only care about pot-bellied pigs, green issues, or the Knights of Columbus – You Sell AVON!

Tag! You're IT with Avon!

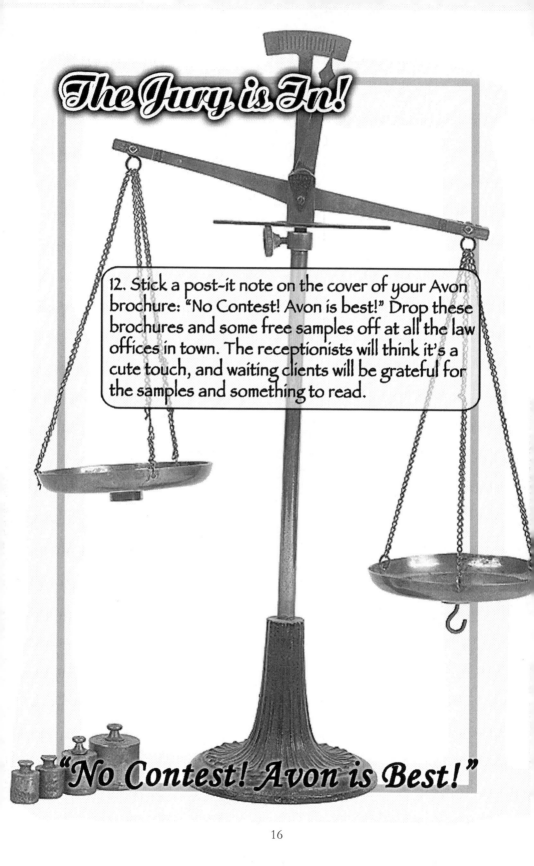

The Jury is In!

12. Stick a post-it note on the cover of your Avon brochure: "No Contest! Avon is best!" Drop these brochures and some free samples off at all the law offices in town. The receptionists will think it's a cute touch, and waiting clients will be grateful for the samples and something to read.

"No Contest! Avon is Best!"

The world is your classroom!

13. Make care packages for all the teachers in town. Include the latest catalogues and samples, plus a few sample-sized products. Include a flier that explains that you offer a 10 percent "Educator's Discount."

"Learn about beauty from Avon"

Be an overnight success with Avon!

14. Hostels – a terrific place to leave those little free Avon samples. Most hostel travelers could use a freshen-up, and will be thankful for the free treat. You would be surprised how many of them are working men and women looking for ways to save on travel costs. After leaving samples in the Santa Fe hostel, I received over 10 orders for items folks left at home or lost along the way, such as deodorants, shampoos, and fragrances. Write across the front of the brochure:

"Avon - the road best traveled"

15. Fast-food cashiers are other workers who are stuck in a booth all day — and most of these workers are women! Write on the cover of your Avon brochure:

"The food is fast, but beauty is eternal!"

Lipstick Cures what Ails You!

16. Your doctor's office is a perfect place to leave some "reading material." If you are leaving a brochure, stuff a couple of your Avon business cards and favorite samples inside the pages. A doctor's office is often an extremely stressful place for folks to wait. A little Avon can cheer up a patient by giving her (or him) something to look forward to. Add a stickie note to the front of your brochures that says:

"Nothing makes you feel more alive than the perfect shade of Avon lipstick!"

A Day at the Beach!

17. Bring your sales literature and samples to the beach or lakeside. Hand out fliers or brochures stamped with:

"They all scream for sunscreen! Ouch! Try Avon SUN Sport!"

Say I Do to Avon!

18. Leave your brochures and samples at Bridal Stores and Tuxedo Rental Stores. Brides, bridesmaids, grooms, and groomsmen want to look their best during the big event! Offer new brides a nice discount if they order Avon to give their Maid of Honor and bridesmaids as a thank you gift. Drop off your Avon brochures and write:

"Take Avon down the isle with you on your special day"

Go Social!

19. Everyone's connecting using Facebook these days! Start a fan page for your Avon business at Facebook.com. Upload photos of your brochures and products, and post daily beauty tips on your Wall. Give customers who "Like" you a discount or an extra sample or two. Make sure to keep your Facebook fan page fresh and exciting! Try posting your favorite skin care regimen or some of the uses you've found for Skin So Soft. Stamp your brochures with:

"Let's Be Friends! Like me on Facebook for exciting updates, discounts, and a first-look at new Avon products!" Don't forget to include your Facebook address!

Drive-by Avoning.

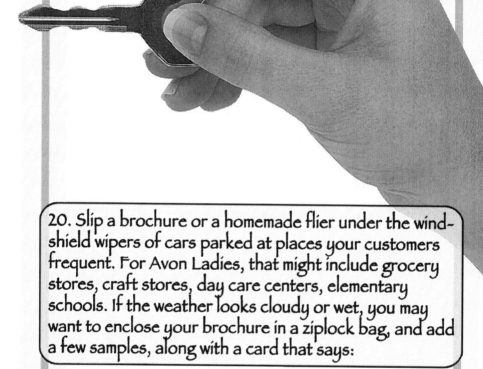

20. Slip a brochure or a homemade flier under the windshield wipers of cars parked at places your customers frequent. For Avon Ladies, that might include grocery stores, craft stores, day care centers, elementary schools. If the weather looks cloudy or wet, you may want to enclose your brochure in a ziplock bag, and add a few samples, along with a card that says:

"While you're driving, you auto know, that Avon's gonna make you glow!"

Story Time

Balls to the Wall

  Last fall, Avon Corporate made a power play. The hell with serving half the world! We're applying phallic logic! They printed thin glossy catalogues featuring items like battery-operated nose hair trimmers and NFL pajamas. A Men's Catalogue, oh baby yeah. And good Avon Lady that I am, I bought in. I ordered two hundred brochures, pictured the fat neighborhood bookkeeper with the closet full of red plaid shirts buying moisturizing face cream and an extra-large spritz bottle of RPM cologne. I might double my earnings, I thought. I might meet a cute single guy in need of soothing eye cream and a soft pair of fingers to apply it. This Men's Catalogue is brilliant, I thought. Brilliant.

  Three months later one hundred fifty Men's Catalogues taunted me from my bedroom floor. No one wanted them. No men sifted through the slick pages, carefully considered the benefits of daily exfoliation. My female customers laughed when I tried to slip them a Men's Catalogue or two to give to the homeboys ruling their sun. You've gotta be kidding, they said. My man barely showers. He ain't gonna start spreading Ab Cream on his love handles. It's a joke, right? I'll just order him that soap-on-a-rope in the regular Avon book.

So I tried stealth brochure drops - leaving those aging books stuck under the windshield wipers of every pickup truck in town, placing one or two next to the girly mags covering the coffee table at the barbershop. But no beauty-hungry men called. My demonstration nose hair trimmers gathered dust. One week before the damn catalogues expired, I still had close to forty glossies littering my floor. Oh crap, I thought. That's fifty cents a book thrown away. I searched the newspaper for some event where men gathered - a demolition derby perhaps, or a bear hunting convention. But Southern California doesn't host a whole lotta manly man get-togethers, so I squished the paper into a small ball. As I reached over my head to toss the wad into the trash, the words Men's Bowling League caught my eye. Oh! This is it! I unwrapped the paper, read the small notice about the winter league finals and nodded my head. Yeah. Bowling. Yeah.

The following Saturday I dressed in my shortest skirt and a yellow-striped Avon tube-top. I applied extra Avon lipstick in 24-Hour Red and lined my eyes with a black Glimmerstick. I spayed as much Avon Advanced Techniques Hair Spray as my dark brown locks could take and added my highest Avon heels. A healthy squirt of Goddess fragrance completed the ensemble. If your regular sales avenues fail, use what ya got, I thought, hiked up my tube top, stuffed those forty Men's Catalogues in my backpack and headed for the bowling alley.

The circulating lights around the Surf Bowl sign seemed to wink at me as I parked in the decaying asphalt drive. I could smell the salt and dead fish of my ocean mixed with the exhaust of a thousand Sunday drivers and the acrid smoke of a group of smokers hiding behind the dumpster. Every time the door opened a waft of sixties surf tunes blew from the alley. The smokers turned in unison to watch me click up the cement stairs. The wind picked up and my skirt rose above my panty line.

No one noticed me walk inside the alley. All eyes were on a string of electronic scoreboards, each displaying a team name across the top and individual players in a neat row along the left-hand side. A team named "Spare Me" rose to their feet with a holler, fists pumping the air as a middle-aged man in a Hawaiian shirt printed with naked hula dancers rolled the pins down, rolled a strike.

Balls to the Wall

They look like good prospects, I thought. Six men sat back down in molded plastic chairs, all late-forties, early-fifties, all in need of some serious men's Avon. A tall man with a shock of gray chest hair escaping from the collar of his Save Our Oceans t-shirt stood, picked up a black ball and stuck two fingers and a thumb in the holes. The track lighting above him bounced off the sheen of the ball, created disco lights on the floor. He twirled around three times as his team-mates chanted "strike, strike, strike, strike," lined the ball to his eye, swung his arm back with a step, let 'er rip. The ball flew from his hand as if it held a hidden magnet, flew straight for the pins, left just two standing. The team lifted beer bottles in unison, tilted heads back and swallowed deep sips. I made my move.

"Hey, guys? Can I sit with you? I have some good luck Avon stuff for you." I didn't wait for an answer, sat cross-legged on the floor at their feet. "Now, guys. Be honest. You wear those bowling shoes all the time, right? How many of you have athlete's feet?" I started opening my backpack to retrieve a handful of samples and a demo tube of Avon Antifungal Foot Cream. The men still held their beer bottles; their mouths open in surprise. "I mean it, guys, I have something that can help. Don't be shy. Speak up!"

A short man with his pants belted far below his stomach clunked his bottle on the floor. "Oh what the hell. I've got athlete's feet." He began to untie his shoes.

"Bob! You're up! Wait and do that later, man!" Hawaiian shirt man pointed to the scoreboard overhead.

"Nah. Maybe she's good luck. Remember the night we snuck the cat in?" The men nodded, looked thoughtful. Bob continued to remove his shoes. I squeezed a generous dollop of cream in his hands and told him to rub it in and around his red toes. I had to breathe through my mouth to avoid smelling them, praying the peppermint and menthol in the product would cover up his nasty foot odor. The men stared at Bob, watched him massage his toes, replace his socks, custom made bowling shoes, stand and grab his ball, a lively glitter green one, and he twirled, they chanted, he rolled....STRIKE!

"Damn. She IS good luck." Hawaiian man pointed to the quietest team member, a shy balding man wearing adventure pants with a million pockets. "Take your shoes off, Fred. The championship is at stake!" He moved his finger from Fred to me, and though he pointed at my head he looked straight at my tube top. "And someone get this lady a beer!"

Between turns, I showed the men my brochures, spritzed each of them with Wild Country cologne, each time at the lane meant another beauty procedure. They covered their hands in Silicon Glove hand cream. They lifted their shirts and applied Mesmerize roll-on deodorant. They bowled like pros, too, one strike after another. Maybe it was the Avon, maybe it was the beer, I didn't know and they didn't care.

"Hell, I'll wear lipstick if our scores keep this up!" Bob stood, prepared to take his turn, look at me expectantly, spoke to my breasts. "So. What's up this time?"

"Uh, we went through all my demo products. I have some Ask Me About Skin So Soft stickers. How about if I stick one on your shirt?" Bob shrugged his shoulders, stuck his chest out. I tried to avoid pressing the sticker onto any stray chest hairs but in Bob's case this was difficult at best. He grabbed his ball and twirled. I looked at my sheet of stickers. Hmmmmmm. I removed another one, stuck it on one of the alley's own balls resting in a tidy row behind me.

"Excuse me? Spare Me Team?" A beefy man with a Surf Bowl manager's shirt and cargo shorts strode toward our lane. "No excess people allowed in the lane during a tournament. This woman must leave." He spat out the word "woman" like I had cooties.

"No way, come on. She's our mascot. Besides the Pin Fall Wizards have a woman at their lane." Hawaiian shirt man opened his arms wide to indicate a group decision. The manager stuck his hands on his hips.

"The Pin Fall Wizards have an infant in one of those - whatchacallit - baby carrier things. That doesn't count!" He pointed at me then pointed at the door. "Out."

I started gathering my leftover materials, started packing demo products and my stickers in my pack. One of the stickers stuck halfway out from the sheet so I removed it and plopped it on another alley ball. The manager's nose turned from red to violet in anger.

"And stop putting stickers on my balls!!!"

Bob lifted his beer. "You wish."

The men exploded in laughter, the manager grabbed my arm, man handled me out the door. But a few days later Hawaiian shirt man called, ordered foot cream and cologne and deodorant for all team members. "Lady, you have no idea how this has changed our game."

"And I bet your wives and girlfriends like the changes too, don't they?" I patted myself on the back, imagined the world a much fresher place with six beautified bowlers.

"Hell, they don't know about this shit. We're only using this stuff during league play."

~ ~ ~

Not-Quite-A-Prank-Call to the Avon Representative Hotline Part One

I wore my trusty duct tape-enhanced backpack filled with Avon brochures as I walked my boys to school this morning. My boys ran ahead, shuffled their feet fast through the new piles of fall leaves. I left five stamped brochures at Gabriel's Filling Station, shoved another two through the Curves womens' workout joint mailslot. I waved goodbye as the boys rounded the school yard, then flipped open my cell phone and hit speed dial #5. The Avon Rep Hotline telephone tree didn't stump me, I knew the click responses by heart, entered my account number, said I had an important product question.

"Hi! Well, I have a question about the Astonishing Lengths mascara. Or any of the mascaras, really. Can they be used on a show terrier?

One of my customers needs to know and I don't know what to tell her."

Silence. I waited two beats. More silence.

"Uh, hello? Did I get disconnected?"

A young boy scooted past me toward the school. His sneakers had tiny wheels embedded underneath a higher than average heel, and he half-walked, half-slided across the uneven brick sidewalk.

"No, ma'am. I'm here. I didn't understand your question. Can you repeat it?"

She spoke with the broad accent of Indiana or Ohio, sounded like she still needed a strong cup of coffee to face the day.

"No problem. Can any of the Avon mascaras be used on a show terrier?"

Silence.

"Ma'am? Did you say snow barrier?"

I laughed.

"No! Show terrier! A show terrier."

I stretched out the words "show" and "terrier" as if they had nineteen syllables each.

"Snow carrier? Is this a joke?"

I could hear her start to move her hands toward the I've-Got-A-Nut-On-The-Line off switch.

"Show terrier! A show dog! A terrier, you know, those whisker faced lap dogs that yap all day? Terrier! Terrier! I need to know if I can slap some mascara on a terrier! For a big show!"

Click. I stared at my cell phone, at the blinking "disconnected" icon, wondered if she would notate my Permanent Record with "likes to make prank calls."

I think I'm going to try again, but I'm scared!

You gotta hand it to Avon!

21. Landscape workers have been some of my most loyal customers. One you demonstrate one of Avon's amazing hand creams – or leave a handful of free Avon samples – they are hooked! Everyone – men and women – wants to have soft, touchable hands. Visit the landfill (more thirsty, calloused hands!), masonry workers, the cemetery (don't laugh – these guys work hard digging those graves!), and the road crews picking up trash and mowing the city parks. Most of these folks have never had anyone give them this kind of gentle attention. You will be amazed at how grateful your new friends will be.

"A rose by any other name... Avon!"

Check out these deals!

22. Hand an Avon brochure to every clerk when you check out. Service workers are always delighted to get something wonderful back from a customer. Make sure to add a sample of a fragrance or lotion.

"What's your TOTAL beauty solution?"

Anti-virus Software for Yourself!

23. Bring a selection of Avon's Anti-Bacterial Hand Gels to your local Internet Cafes. You are sure to convince the proprietor that keeping the computers germ-free will help business, especially during flu season!

"Don't take an internet virus home with you! Use Avon!"

High Performance (Bath) Oil

24. Tape a brochure or flier to the coin-input slot at your local carwash, along with the list of Skin So Soft uses. This miracle bath oil works great on cars, too! Tagline:

"Make your car a real beauty with Avon's Skin So Soft – removes nearly everything from your car's finish!"

Over-Indulged?

25. Be creative! Visit the sports bars in your town. Make a flier that says "Treat the Woman in Your Life" and feature a list of the hottest Avon fragrances, fashions, and jewelry. Sometimes men stay out a little later than they should. What a great way to get back into favor at home! Ask the bartender if you can leave your fliers and cards with him or her.

"Treat the Woman in Your Life"

Blog it, Baby!

26. That's how I reached Honor Society in just one year! I started a blog where I posted daily beauty tricks, reviews of Avon products, and Before & After photos showing the wonderful results you can achieve using Avon's skin care line. You can start a free blog at blogger.com or wordpress.com. Update your blog a couple times a week to keep it fresh and inviting and to keep your customers coming back for more.

Use 'Avon' in the blog title to get more search engine hits!

You Won't Get Lost in the Woods With Avon!

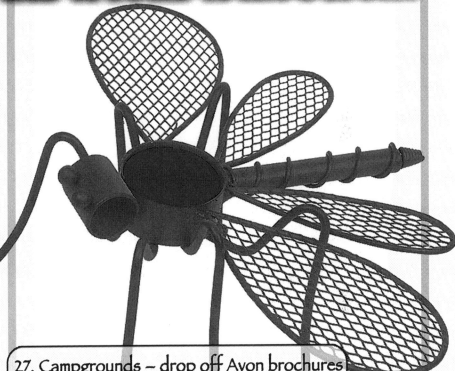

27. Campgrounds – drop off Avon brochures and samples or demo products of SUN Sport sunscreen and Bug Guard insect-repellent. Laminate a copy of your "100 Ways to use Skin so Soft" and ask the camp ranger if you can hang it in the bathroom. Write on the cover of your Avon brochure:

"Skin so Soft – a real knockout for bugs!"

'On call' makeup artist!

28. Movie Theatres! Leave a business card, Avon brochure, samples on your theatre seat, in the restrooms, next to the video games, hand them to the concession workers. Be sure to tag them with:

"Let Avon make you a star!"

or

"Everyone's a star. Who does YOUR makeup?"

Inside and Out!

29. Chiropractic patients are usually in pain! Leave a stack of fliers, Avon brochures, and samples, and add this line to your literature in big, bold print:

"Now that you're back is cracked, treat yourself to a soothing Avon bubble bath tonight."

Avon knows beauty to a tee!

30. Golf Courses – another great place to leave that sunscreen and bug-repellent! Some fancier courses have powder rooms for the ladies. Drop your Avon brochures here and write:

"Let Avon be your caddie on the greens"

Go Social!

31. One of the hottest new social networks is Google +. Create an Avon Customer "circle" at Google + and add your customers - new and old - to the circle. Update your new Avon circle with specials, brochure deadlines, special offers, and discounts. Add other Google + users to your Avon circle.

Business online is just like business in "real" life - don't forget to thank folks for following your Google + updates by offering a free sample or a product special.

Red or White?

32. Vintner's and wine tasting events are a great place to subtly hand other attendees one of your Avon business cards. One the back, hand-write:

*"Red or White?
Avon has all your colors."*

Pearly whites deserve pearls!

33. Leave a brochure at your Dental or Orthodontic office. Add a stapled business card to the cover that states:

"Now that your teeth are straight and white, add some Avon jewels tonight!"

Introduce Yourself!

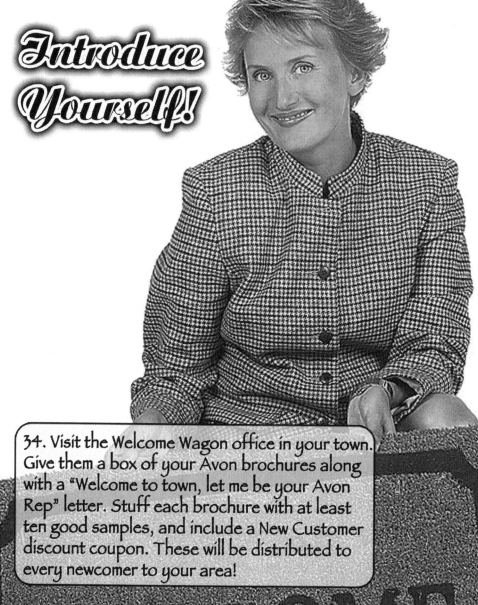

34. Visit the Welcome Wagon office in your town. Give them a box of your Avon brochures along with a "Welcome to town, let me be your Avon Rep" letter. Stuff each brochure with at least ten good samples, and include a New Customer discount coupon. These will be distributed to every newcomer to your area!

"Welcome to town, Let me be your Avon Rep!"

Meet your community with beauty!

35. The community rooms and pool areas of apartment and condo complexes usually have a table and a bulletin board for residents' use. Pin up your Avon flier, and place your Avon books and cards on the table. Always cover both bases – flier and brochure – when you can.

"Your apartment needs a key – and so does your beauty: Avon!"

Write about it!

36. Like to write? Craft a column for your local newspaper solving a local and timely problem - Skin So Soft for bug control during the summer, or how to look your best for a job interview. Make sure to mention that you also sell Avon in your column, and provide a tag line at the end with your telephone number or email address. Newspapers are always looking for fun content. You might want to write several columns and offer a selection of news to get through the fall, spring, summer, and winter. Articles that can help readers get through these tough economic times would be especially appreciated.

Column ideas? How about: Smile Your Way to Success, Inexpensive & Natural Flea Control, or Freshen Your Wardrobe with New Lipstick.

Facepainting for Mom!

37. Day care centers are wonderful places to drop some Avon brochures. Sometimes I make a special delivery with colorful helium balloons tied with curly ribbons, an Avon book tied to the end of the ribbon as a weight. Add a cute card with these words:

"What about YOU, baby! Moms need care, too!"

'A' is for Avon!

39. Slip your Avon cards into books and magazine in bookstores, and in the books and mags you see at the grocery, convenience store, and airport shops. Write on the back of your cards:

"Next Chapter – Chapped Lips Solutions"

Reel 'em In!

40. Have a fishing hole or lake in your area? Drop by on a sunny Saturday morning and give the fishermen and women Avon brochures and discount coupons for SUN Sport suncreen and Bug Guard insect-repellent. Your tagline:

"Make sure the fish are the only ones biting with Avon Bug Guard."

Tips of the Trade

Here are three fun ways I get my brochures opened by my potential customers:

1. Make your Avon brochures part of the local news!

Is your customer a mom of school-aged children? Tape the weekly lunch menu to the front of the brochure! If she (or he) is a sports nut, tape the local teams' schedules to the book.

The list here is endless - timely, useful bits of news and local goings on will give your Avon customer an incentive to open your brochure. I usually include more information inside - the weekly weather report, a list of cultural events.

I can't tell you how many times my Avon customers thank me for this information! In fact, they begin to rely on it! They will look for that biweekly brochure so that they will know what the Middle School is serving Tuesday for hot lunch!

2. Surprise your potential customer with a bit of adult intrigue...

You can wrap your brochure in plain construction paper, and then add a funny joke or saying to the cover. Your potential customer won't know what to think! It is some kind of new, strange adult magazine?! She will have a great laugh when she rips open the paper cover and discovers an Avon brochure. If you've added a personalized note under the paper cover, I guarantee she'll keep opening and opening.

3. Make your customer laugh with a little bit of kid humor!

I often add "googly eyes" to the cover of my brochure, especially when the cover shot is a beautiful model. I glue googly craft eyes over the pupils of Ms. Perfect, and then add a funny caption underneath.

Your customer will open that book! She will want to know what ELSE you might have done!

The Great Homemade AVON Business Card Experiment

A few weeks ago I grabbed a handful of blank business cards. I have printed cards, too, ones with my name and address and number and Avon Representative in ten-point Helvetica. I wanted to create something a little different, though, something unusual, something that would catch a potential customer's eye and imagination.

I spread out an assortment of old, wrinkled Avon brochures - ones that were too tatty and soiled to hand out or leave in my usual haunts. I thumbed through the pages and ripped out sayings like "Reduction in Wrinkles" and "New Colors" and "100% of women noticed improved skin texture." I kept the raw edges, pasted them to the blank cardstock with rubber cement. I added carefully scissored eyes, lips, gorgeous hands. I added quirk, funny quotes of my own. "I can help you!" "I'm your AVON connection!"

I taped a sample to the back, added my name and contact info in a bright color, dropped them here and there. Probably spent three hours all told on the experiment.

This morning I got the first call from those crazy cards. A man. A business owner who needs emergency Avon for some employees, a New Year's gift. 400 bucks worth. He said he likes my style.

And believe me, this order came at the perfect time.

Tips of the Trade

Insert Beauty Tip Cards in Your Avon Brochures

Here's something new I am trying this week, with the thought that it might help potential customers try a new product:

I printed out six different sets of Beauty Tips - each covering one topic, just enough information to fit on a piece of cardstock the same size as a regular Avon brochure. I slipped one card inside each brochure, making sure it sits in the pages where the product is featured.

This week's card will feature Blush! Here's the info I printed out on these cards:

How to apply blush to flatter facial shape:

Don't try to "contour" your face with darker and lighter shades of blush; that's "pro" territory. Simply apply regular blush with your face shape in mind.

On a round face, place blush from the center of your cheek, out along the ridge of your cheekbone, blending upward towards your temples. Dot some on your chin, too.

On a square face, use minimal blush placed on the lower apple of your cheek. Don't sweep it upwards or to the side.

On a narrow face, blush goes at the outer point of your cheekbone. Don't sweep it upwards; keep it horizontal.

Make the Most of your eRep Site!

Every Avon Representative has the opportunity to use his or her Avon eRep site to build a lasting and vibrant business.

Did you know:

You can live chat with potential customers at your eRep site, and even choose whether to chat in English or Spanish!

You can create an individual Beauty Profile for each of your customers, whether you service them online or in person.

You can set up Online Events and E-Parties and even hold more than one at the same time! Offer special customers great deals or provide a fundraiser for your favorite organizations.

You can even set up your own Avon eRep website with a blog and keep customers up-to-date on your opinions, reviews, thoughts, and beauty tips.

Your own personal eRep site – which comes with your kit when you sign on to be an Avon Representative – allows you to manage your inventory, customers, and calendar with ease. Be sure to make the most of it!

Here are some easy ways to get more folks to find your Avon eRep site:

1. Make as many FREE websites or blogs as you like and link them to your eRep site.

2. Set up a Facebook fan page for your eRep site.

3. Make sure you Tweet your eRep site each campaign.

4. Comment on Beauty Blogs, leaving your eRep URL. Be a good Net Citizen and be sure to leave a thoughtful comment – no one likes spam!

5. Always print your eRep URL on your business card and on each brochure. Some customers love the privacy of ordering from their own home.

10 Easy Ways to be an Environmentally Friendly Avon Representative

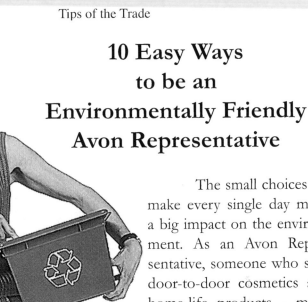

The small choices we make every single day make a big impact on the environment. As an Avon Representative, someone who sells door-to-door cosmetics and home-life products - many of them in disposable containers - I worry about how much my actions negatively contribute to our planet's well-being. I have made a conscious effort to lessen my own personal as well as Avon business environmental impact, by following these easy ideas:

1. Pull the plug on electronics and chargers. Any Avon electronic device (nose hair trimmers, anyone?) as well as cell phones, iPods, digital cameras and other devices use energy, even if they are turned off, if the charger is still plugged in.

2. Don't idle that engine! If you are delivering products to your Avon customers, turn off your car engine and handle your business without allowing your car to waste precious fuel.

3. Recycle those Avon delivery bags! I have a program with my local customers called the "Green Avon Bag" project. Each regular customer who wishes to participate gives me a cloth grocery bag with her name written across the bottom in indelible ink. I fill with her ordered products, deliver the goods, and she hangs the bag outside for me to collect during my next rounds. I've saved money on those expensive Avon delivery bags, and my customers and I are happy knowing we helped save trees!

Avon, are you listening to that last idea? You could produce cute multiple-use cloth bags that customers can purchase and use over and over! Your loyal reps AND customers alike would purchase these, knowing they were helping save trees and preserving landfill space.

4. Use recycled paper for your customer newsletters and invoices! Recycle old Avon brochures, too, instead of throwing them away. Cut out photos of products to make your own mini-adverts. Stamp the brochure with "Yes, I'm Out of Date, but I'm Still HOT!" and then honor the older prices.

5. Turn your Avon trash into crafts! Empty and cleaned skin-care tubs make great paper-clip holders and paint wells for kids' crafts. Use your imagination and reuse some of these plastic items.
6. Ride your bike or walk when you make your Avon rounds. Great exercise, too!

7. Check the numbers on the bottom of plastic products. On the bottom of every plastic product, (including Avon lotion and cream bottles, soda and water bottles, contact lenses, etc.), there is a number printed that corresponds to the kind of plastic used. If there is no number, the item isn't recyclable.

8. Use rechargeable batteries when you are demo-ing any Avon electronic item.

9. Steer away from disposable cups and bring your own mug! Get your District Sales Manager to stop buying throw-away cups for those monthly meetings. Use washable mugs, and encourage your downline, upline, and local Avon Rep friends to bring their own mugs to meetings and set a good example!

10. I'm going to take a little heat on this suggestion, but it's something I highly encourage my own customers to do: Buy wisely. Use your 'purchasing power' to reject products with excessive packaging and buy goods that last, not disposable products such as one-use wipes. I don't care if this impacts my bottom line.

 These ten ideas are simple, and truth be told nothing new, but if each of us can better tend the circle of energy surrounding us, we will create concentric circles that spill across the globe. It's up to each one of us to save this planet!

Go to the Dogs!

41. Feed stores, pet stores, boarding kennels, and farm suppliers are a wonderful place to leave a Skin So Soft flier (See the end of this book for over 100 uses of Skin So Soft!) listing all the bath oil's amazing uses including as a flea-repellent, a massage oil for your cat, dog, pot-bellied pig, horse, or goat. Your flier can say:

"Give your pet a new leash on life with Avon Skin So Soft!"

Leave Your Stamp!

42. Leave a brochure for your mail carrier. You can hang it off of your mailbox — never inside the box as that is a violation of federal law. Drop a sample or two of Moisture Therapy hand cream inside the brochure — your mail carrier spends hours a day sorting and delivering mail with her hands! Write across the front of the brochure:

"You've got mail..."

Q(ucik) R(esponse) with Avon!

43. Create a QR Code for your Avon e-rep site! A QR Code is a square pixelated design that you can scan, using your smart phone or computer tablet such as an iPad. It will automatically take the customer to your e-rep site! You can add a sticker with the code to the back of your Avon brochures, or add the square design to your business cards. Get on the smart phone train today!

Get 'Smart' with Avon!

Be the First to the Finish Line!

44. Avon where they work AND play! NASCAR races are popular with men and women these days! Hand out Avon brochures labeled with:

"Get your lip gloss up to speed!"

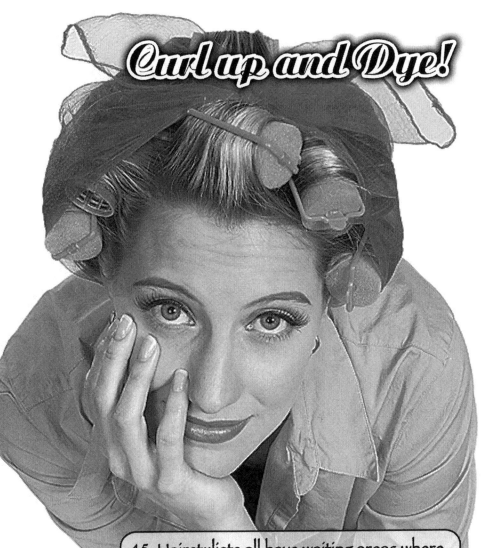

Lost Luggage?

46. Most cities and large towns have a Tourist information center or booth. Drop off a stack of fliers with a list of products a traveler to your town might need. Ideas:

"Forget sunscreen? Call me for Avon SUN Sport!"

"Traveling? Call me for quality men's and women's toiletries!"

Cheese or The Works?

47. Pizza take-out waiting areas – leave your business cards near the free penny pincher newspapers. Look for a community bulletin board to post your flier. Add the line:

"Don't look cheesy! Call me for beauty tips!"

Beauty is its own Pitch!

48. Every sports season holds Avon opportunity! Attend the local soccer, baseball, basketball, and football games. Parents come out in droves to watch their children play – and you can hand them a brochure and sample. Your tagline:

"Step up to the plate with Avon!"

Avon answers your beauty calls!

49. Have a telephone call center or other phone-based service center in your area? The people that work at these locations often end up with sore, calloused hands from the constant telephone work. Bring hand cream samples and Avon brochures and hand them out as they exit their workplace at the end of the day. You don't even need to say anything! If you hold your hand out with free samples, you won't be turned down very often. Always, always offer a New Customer discount. Write on the cover of your Avon brochure:

"Call ME!"

Unlock Tax Time!

51. Make a flier with the header: "Beauty is the Best Return!" and drop these off along with some samples at the Tax Preparation Centers in town. Taxes are another stressful situation for most people, and a little free sample can bring a smile and a potential sale.

"Beauty is the Best Return"

Go Social!

52. Get a Twitter account for your Avon business at twitter.com. Twitter allows you to update your followers with a 140 character sentence as many times a day as you like! Put your Twitter name on your Avon business card and on all brochures and offer daily tips and hints, mentioning Avon products, of course! Offer your customers a one-time discount or a free lip balm if they sign up to become your Twitter follower.

Here's a sample tweet: Is winter stealing your hair's lustre? Try Avon Advanced Techniques Lotus Shield for shiny, soft, gorgeous locks!

Congrats on a NEW life!

53. Call your local hospital's Maternity Ward and ask if you can bring them some New Mom Diaper Bags. Find tote bags at the dollar store and fill them with the current and upcoming Avon brochures, a large selection of samples, and a couple of trial sized products such as lip balms, bath oil, and hand creams. Let the world know:

"The stork delivers babies, but I deliver beauty!"

Exercise your beauty options with Avon!

54. Dance studios, yoga studios, Pilates studios – all exercise locations could use a little of your Avon TLC. Leave lipstick samples in the changing rooms, along with some of Avon's hot new fragrance samples! Write across the front of the brochure:

"Stretch your beauty budget with Avon"

In the Bag!

55. After you load your groceries in your car, return the grocery cart and leave a brochure in the basket. You can leave brochures in hand baskets, too!

"Don't leave beauty off your list!"

Avon is Sew nice!

56. Fabric Stores are full of wonderful seamstresses who need Avon for those busy, chapped hands. Find out when your local store holds sewing classes, and drop by with brochures and samples for all students.

"Trim your beauty budget with Avon!"

Why not have the Smell of Success?

57. Leave recruiting brochures and sales brochures at the local Unemployment office. You can arrive early in the morning when most folks arrive to check the job openings and hand them out in person, too. On your fliers:

"Look as good as your resume sounds!"

Knit One, Purl Two.

58. Read the event listings in your local paper. Place Avon brochures and samples in a pretty gift basket and drop it off at the start of each event. Works great for knitting groups, book clubs, wedding and baby showers – any event where your potential customers congregate. Attending a knitting group? Add this tagline to your flier or Avon brochure:

"When Knit Happens, Avon is there!"

Don't leave home without it!

59. Bus stops! Train stations! Leave a couple of brochures on the bus or train, too, with the added line in big, bold colorful print:

*"Beauty:
Getting there is easy with Avon!"*

Race to the finish!

60. Gas station workers for self-serve and full-serve stations need Avon! You're out of gas, and they are out of gel! Hand them a brochure and samples, and perhaps demo a beautifully-fragranced hand cream to counteract the smell of oil and gas. On your brochure:

"Rev up your engine with Avon!"

Story Time

Jesucristo

Hmmm, I thought. That gives me an idea. I faced my computer again, and opened a new document.

Avon Wing-Ding-O-Rama!
Free Makeovers!
Free Cookies and Drinks!
See the NEW Avon Products!
Meet a REAL Avon Lady!!!!!

I liked the last line the best. At the bottom I listed my address, the nearest cross street and the date and hours of the event — two weeks in advance. I printed out thirty copies on large paper and a set of rainbow fliers, and spritzed them all with the most ghastly overpowering perfume Avon sold. I drew a scarlet-red lipstick kiss around the prose, as if the invitation floated out of the puckered mouth of a wanton woman. I pressed colored felt-tip markers against sheets of blank labels and printed "13 Hours of Madness" along with my telephone number and the date of the event.

I closed my eyes and attempted to conjure up ideas for my weekend Avon yard sale. Maybe I should offer face painting for kids? Maybe create some kind of free raffle for one of the new products? I imagined my Avon Open House Wing-Ding-O-Rama, at the top of the patchwork cul-de-sac with assorted children gun-running lemonade and peanut butter cookies and one lone short grumpy middle-aged bastard of a neighbor three houses down, peering out behind tasteful beige drapes, hoping I'd use too much Avon fade cream and disappear with the orange sun before any fireworks start. I crossed my fingers and hoped at the end of the sale I wouldn't see him laughing at the sight of me jilted at the Avon altar.

I called the local paper and placed an ad for my yard sale. 13 Hours of Avon Madness! Free beauty consultations and makeovers! Free Avon samples! Incredible sale on products! Petting zoo for the kids! Come one, come all! Saturday, 7 am – 8 pm.

I dropped Louie and Marty at a community art class and headed for my favorite neighborhood, a swirl of busy cul-de-sacs of identical cream stucco spaces where I would never want to live, but boy, do they buy a lot of Avon. I left a brochure with every housekeeper and soccer mom and landscape artist and grannie and cook and stray child. I passed out handmade stickers that read "13 Hours of Madness" and my telephone number and the date. One boy pulling a skateboard by a fraying dirty piece of rope took two stickers and stuck them under his board next to a skull and what looked like a satanic symbol.

My sale began at seven a.m. sharp, but I started getting ready at six. I set out two card tables with demonstration products and handheld mirrors. I stacked two sets of two Avon delivery boxes side by side and laid an eight-foot section of particle board over them, covering it with a red and green plastic Christmas tablecloth and plates of homemade cookies, a bowl of cheese doodles, a pitcher of lemonade and fifty Sponge Bob Dixie cups. My sons, Louie and Marty, placed metal folding chairs here and there, and I banished the dog to the house where she sat, wet nose pressed against the front window, wishing she were human and carefree. I set out brochures, order forms, all the samples I possessed, and created a kids' play section in one corner of the driveway with the Avon Wellness Yoga Mat and the Avon Cardio Slide.

Frankie, the stray come-to-stay pot-bellied pig, stood in the playpen. One of the aluminum legs was loose so I shored it up with duct tape. Louie made a Petting Zoo sign and fastened it to the mesh sides. I tied a dozen rainbow balloons to my mailbox and sat down to wait.

And wait. And wait. And wait.

At ten-thirty I was still waiting. Marty, Louie and six neighborhood kids sat in a circle next to the fitness equipment, playing Duck, Duck, Goose, and eating what remained of the cookies and lemonade. Frankie gave a soulful look to any child who glanced his way, hoping for a cookie. I watched middle-aged neighbors mow lawns, prune trees, travel to and fro with groceries and surfboards. They waved at me, their crazy cohabitant Avon Lady, happy I was home to watch all their children, not grateful enough to sit on my lawn and flip through a brochure.

A tiny girl with raven hair and her mother's unusual stretchy mouth left the circle and pointed to the makeup samples. "Can you put some on me?"

Why not? No one else was running up my hilly street for some blush and a bit of eyeliner. I ran my hand along the pile of miniature lipsticks looking for something simple and innocent, but Goth Girl grabbed the most virulent of the reds. "This one!"

So I shaded her lips as lightly as I could with Reckless Red. I added a touch of Shimmering Gleam Creme to her cheeks and eyelids and patted her arms with fragrant Timeless bath powder. She stared in a handheld mirror, studying the shape of her lips. As I reached for a black Glimmerstick - I wanted to draw in a fake beauty mark on her left cheek - the short grumpy man three doors down opened his garage and his killer dachshund yipped and flew straight for my herd of duck duck geese.

"AaaaaaaEEeeeeeeEEEEeeeeAAaaaaaaa!!!!!!!!!!!!" The screams of eight children rang through the court as the hotdog jumped for either the plate of cookie crumbs or the bowl of cheese doodles. The plates went one way, the kids went another, the particle board fell off the boxes, into the grass, into the dog, lemon halves and orange doodles flying through the air like a flotilla of miniature UFOs. And Little Miss Goth screaming, screaming for life, for fun, for the terror of it, because of the spastic hyper pooch, because she was outside and red and shiny and five years old. And then she dropped the mirror, crash, clang, shatter, into a thousand shards of bad luck on the drive.

But that wasn't the worst of it, oh no. Louie decided we needed paper towels and brooms and a trash can to clean up this mess of an Avon sale, and he snuck away from the commotion and ran into the house, the house containing the big white sissy dog who stood watching the shrimpy Hound of Baskervilles wanna-be tear through HER YARD, and she tore past Louie, through the door, and sailed into the front yard with a tousle of fur and fleas and anger and justice and growled straight for the dachshund. I dove for Suzie and grabbed her by the collar but she didn't let up, and I fell to the ground like a pancake, flat on my belly, Suzie dragging me three feet or more until she gave up and plopped on the ground, head between two sad paws. Frankie sat still in his playpen. He gave us a sad look as if he'd seen messes like this in the past.

I stood, blood oozing from my right arm, the side of my right thigh like raw hamburger, and carried my heavy dumb dog back into the house, cleaned my wounds, took a hundred deep breaths, and wished for those days back in the neighborhood of my youth, where we lived for sneaking out at night and drinking Schlitz Malt Liquor Bull down at the dock.

When I came back outside, I saw eight little kids sweeping the driveway, picking up broken plates and bottles of Skin-So-Soft and those thousand beauty samples, trying to arrange them just so on the particle board now cracked down the middle and tilted like a canoe, covered in dirty Christmas wrapping. My grumpy neighbor walked toward me, the man who once, eight months ago, stood in the street and pointed at me and my house and called it a clown house, an embarrassment, called me a white-trash woman with loose morals, called me things ten times worse. He walked with hands in pockets, his perpetual motion hotdog back in his yard, and I braced for another barrage of weary insult.

"Sorry 'bout that. Whatcha selling?" He looked at me through brown eyes trying to be kind through his hard edge, and I noticed for the first time in five years that he had beautiful wavy black hair. He bought two bottles of bug lotion and ordered a sunscreen. He wrote me a check then and there, and I was afraid to tell him no, you don't pay until it arrives.

Slowly, other customers arrived, one by lone one, a couple here, a couple there. Most were women I met in their homes, stopping by to gossip and get a free sample or two. Several women placed orders for makeup and skin care items. Two Latina ladies stopped at the table, looked at the brochures, chose a lipstick each, and waved thank you. I raised my arm to wave in return.

"Jesucristo!" Both women invoked Jesus' name and made the sign of the cross. I turned around to see what the heck was happening now, but nothing but my messy driveway and garage door stared back at me. The women spoke excitedly in Spanish and left my yard in a hurry. I saw them gesturing with arms and hands, squishing into a two door Toyota Celica with a dented engine hood. I stood with hands on hips, wondering what made them run, when I heard a voice I remembered, a voice I'd heard twice in my Avon past.

"So where's your kilt, lassie?" The man who questioned what was under said kilt stood at the end of the drive with a woman on his arm. She towered over him by at least three inches, placing her well above six-feet tall. Her hair cascaded down her shoulders in golden waves, movie star hair, and she laughed in a low knowing tone at her companion's question. "I saw your note and had to see what you'd do next. Here, show Eliza what you're selling." He took a chair next to the exercise station and rested his elbows on his knees, looking over the wreckage with that same sardonic grin. I showed Eliza around the three tables, gave her colors and powders and creams in little sample packettes, gave her brochures and printed fliers. I peppered her with questions, tried to find out if she was his wife or girlfriend or sister.

"Ha Ha, did your friend tell you how I threw some lipsticks at him a few weeks ago?" I hoped the word 'friend' would be enough bait but Eliza just snickered. She placed an order for a blush, a powder, a powder puff, and two Glimmersticks, and left her address, a house across town from Kilt Man's place. They left together, arm-in-arm, laughing, walking slowly like good pals or lovers, perhaps both.

When all was said and done and cleaned and put away and laid to rest, Alleluia and Amen, I stripped in the bathroom, ready to take a long, hot Avon-scented bubble bath. My ripped-up thigh caught my eye, and then I turned my arm to look at the damage there. Jesucristo, indeed! The sure face of Jesus, complete with bleeding thorns, peered out from my skin.

That is, if I squinted a little and I flexed the triceps just so.

Jaworski

Birdie Jaworski
nt Sales Rep

November 8, 2011

Dear ,

If your organization needs to raise money, instead of selling candy, wrapping paper or T-shirts, why not consider Avon! Avon has been assisting organizations such as yours in their successful fund-raising for several years. Your organization can earn 40% profit on products for the whole family: beauty products, insect repellents, sun lotion, bubble bath, gifts and much, much more. Plus, with an Avon Fund-raiser:

- ☐ Your organization will be selling popular products that have a world wide reputation for quality
- ☐ Every customer your organization sells to will be satisfied- because every Avon product has a money-back guarantee.
- ☐ I can work with you to create a custom- designed fund-raiser: You sell what you want, when you want, how you want.
- ☐ There's minimal investment from your organization- with profits paid directly and immediately to you!

I would like to have the opportunity to meet personally with you to show you a sampling of Avon products and fun- raising materials. We can then determine what type of fund-raiser would work best for your organization

If you have any immediate questions, please call me at xxx-xxx-xxxx. I will be calling you within a few days to schedule an appointment to talk about how Avon can become partners with you in developing a successful fund- raising event. I look forward to meeting with you soon.

Sincerely,

Birdie Jaworski
Avon Independent Sales Representative

For all your Avon Needs!!
Birdie Jaworski, Avon Independent Sales Rep.

First class beauty with Avon!

61. Airport waiting areas are great places to leave more "reading material" and skin care samples. Leave your youravon.com e-Rep information so that any traveler can order from you from anywhere in the world On your fliers:

"Take flight with our beauty specials!"

Fast Response with Avon!

62. Leave brochures and samples at the Police Station. Police officers are hard workers, and often have dry hands or lines around their eyes due to stress. Offer to bring samples for the entire force - you will always feel protected! On your brochure:

"Getting beat from your beat? Try Avon!"

Wake up to Avon!

63. Coffee Shops often have bulletin boards where customers can post fliers and business cards. This is a perfect opportunity for you to carefully cut out a few special pages out of the current brochure and tack them to the board. Circle your favorite products. Add a cute line:

"Freshen your lipstick on me - call for free lipstick sample!"

Manage your life with Avon!

64. Property management companies often have to show rental properties. Bring them the latest Avon brochures where you have highlighted home care items that can help any rental look and smell wonderful. Skin so Soft can impart a gorgeous shine to cabinets and give a lovely smell to any restroom.

"Get a new Lease on life with Avon!"

Hands on.
Hands down.
Avon means beauty!

65. Massage therapists and other bodywork professionals can become great customers for skin care products. Drop off brochures and samples for products they would use in their practice.

"With Avon, beauty can be more than skin deep"

Stuck in the Spin Cycle?

66. Potential customers are all around you! Stack your brochures on the folding tables of local Laundromats, and add the tagline:

"Try Skin So Soft - your skin would like a little 'fabric' softener too!"

Take your business to the third dimension!

YouTube

67. Start an Avon Representative YouTube Channel at YouTube.com and film yourself applying the latest skin care products or demonstrating the hottest Mark jewelry and handbags. Take suggestions from your audience on what videos they would like you to see! It can be difficult to figure out what products look like from a two dimensional paper brochure. Video can bring the beauty of Avon to life!

You are the Star of Avon!

"Bingo!" Avon calling!

68. Most churches have social events such as potluck dinners, lectures, Bingo, rummage sales, etc. Bring your brochures and samples to these events. You can either ask if there is a place for you to leave them for others to enjoy, or you can mingle with the crowd and hand them out one by one. Your tagline for a bingo night:

"Avon has your number!"

Skate to Success!

69. Skating rinks! Leave your brochures and samples in the café area as well as the places where parents watch their chilren skate. Ideas for your fliers:

"Nails as hard as ICE!"

Look sharp. Think sharp!

70. Have a college campus in your town? Leave your Avon brochures and samples in the dormitories, communal eating areas, lecture halls, administrative offices. Consider offering students a discount if they collect orders from their friends.

"Make the grade with Avon!"

Give the old a new sense of beauty with Avon!

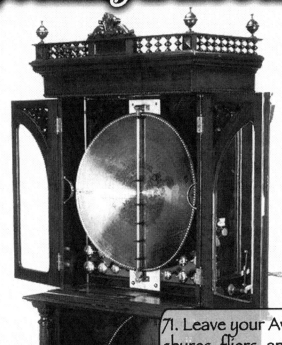

71. Leave your Avon brochures, fliers, and samples at flea markets and antique shows. Did you know that Skin so Soft can impart a gorgeous sheen to wood furniture? Bring a demonstration bottle and spritz dusty dressers. You will have grateful clients!

"Taking care of appearances never goes out of style!"

Save a space for Avon!

72. Parking lot attendants run around all day moving and retrieving cars. Don't discount any of these professions – even if the worker is a man, he needs personal care supplies, and he may have a girlfriend, and he certainly has a mother! On your brochure:

"Avon: Your personal beauty valet!"

Bargain Hunting?

73. County fairs, flea markets, antique shows – anywhere people meet to purchase or sell junk. Both the vendors and attendees are potential customers for you. Make a special brochure with this heading:

"Clearing out your closet? Let me help bring some new color into your life!"

Take Center Stage!

74. Bring Avon business cards with a free sample taped to the back to Rock concerts. Stamp them with: "Rock & Roll on some Avon deodorant, baby!" Opera? For a night attending Bizet's "*Les Pêcheurs de Perles*," stamp them with "Throw on some Avon Pearlesque jewels!" Country concert? Stamp your cards with "Get your Dolly on with Avon!"

"Rock and Roll on some Avon deodorant, baby!"

Avon pays big beauty dividends!

75. Insert your business card into the payment envelope when you send in your bills! The women and men to open your payments will be thrilled with the diversion! Enclose a page from an upcoming brochure with an Avon hand cream or fragrance circled. A sample is nice to include, too.

"Avon saves your skin!"

Don't horse around - choose Avon!

76. County fairs are wonderful places to leave Avon brochures and samples. Skin so Soft can be used to soften and add shine to a horse's or goat's coat. Leave a large spray bottle of Skin so Soft - labeled with your name & number, of course - in the show barn.

"Don't let dry hands get your goat - Skin so Soft saves the day!"

Clean Up with Avon!

77. Housecleaning services usually use fairly harsh chemicals and bleaches to clean their clients' homes. Why not drop by their sales office and drop off a flier describing the many uses of Skin So Soft, along with a small discount coupon? On your fliers:

"Polish and shine yourself!"

Sponsor your local station!

78. Donate Avon to your local NPR station for their twice-a-year fund drive giveaways. NPR stations love these kinds of donations, and will read your name and business number over the air as a generous sponsor. How about putting together several gift baskets for the drive? Or a selection of Avon jewelry?

Next Ten Callers Get Avon!

Feeling Spooky?

79. Give out Avon at Halloween! Hand an Avon sample to the parents as you drop a goodie in the Trick or Treaters' bags. Make sure you have samples for both men and women! Fragrance, mini lipsticks, and skin care trials are all great ways to say Happy Halloween!

There's no trick to this treat!

On the Radio!

80. Like to talk? Try your local radio station! Offer to come on the air and answer callers questions about beauty. Or offer to give a once a week "Beauty Tip." Perhaps your local station has a feature program where they interview community business owners. Make sure to speak clearly and remember to give your listeners a way to contact you after the show. It's always a good idea to offer a coupon code or special offer for listeners.

Make Radio Waves With Avon!

Product Reviews: Know your Avon!

When I started selling and blogging about Avon, something strange happened, something I didn't expect. I started experimenting with my Avon goodies and discovered I liked a lot of them! Not all of them, mind you, but enough to keep me interested, keep me telling potential customers and my two blog readers that I kinda liked Avon. Avon is OK, I posted.

I tested a few more items. I wrote truthful reviews - some of them positive, some of them bad. More visitors came to sit at my blog, wait for another piece of my puzzle. I knocked on more doors. I sold more product. I met people with pasts, with character, with bushy eyebrows and a million pet cats. I told their stories, told about my Avon connection to them.

Selling Avon gave me determination and a reason to open my mouth, and the wider I opened, the more flies I captured, the more wings and legs I spit on the digital page. I became a spider with a web, but I let my prey go, let them read my stories and reviews and make decisions for themselves. I expected a hand slap from Avon HQ, expected my independent rep pink slip and a letter explaining how I was doing Avon wrong. It never came. We love you, District Managers wrote. We love your stories, the Avon call center employees posted.

Two years later I field a few hundred inquiries a week. Tell me about Avon, they ask, tell me about the products, tell me whether I should sell it, too. Yeah, I tell them, every one of them. Give it a try.

Avon gave me a reason to connect to humanity, a reason to extend my hand to touch another person. Avon gave me a backpack of glamour, and though my skin glows pink and my legs are soft and smooth, the real beauty happens every time I knock on a door and a new person answers.

Please enjoy my collection of reviews of the most popular Avon products. At the end you will find two short, funny stories!

Review of Avon Solutions Ageless Results Night Cream:

Hot damn! I love, love, love times a million this product! This is my new catchall night cream. I use it every night since it hit the Avon scene, and it leaves my skin looking better, firmer, softer, clearer, than it does with ANY of the other Avon night creams and specialty creams. It smells nice, it smoothes gently into my skin and doesn't leave a tight or greasy feel. It's only $15.00, too, much less than half the price of the Anew Clinical creams. The best part? It doesn't give me whopper zits!

The advertising for this product sits next to three smiling sexy dermatologists in the Avon brochure, and proudly proclaims that "100% of women showed improvements in signs of aging... shouldn't you?" Add me to the proud 100%. All of my customers love this line of products, too.

I also love the Avon Solutions Ageless Results Day Cream, which is the companion product and contains 15 SPF. The Avon Solutions Ageless Eye Cream is also lovely, and leaves my eyes feeling pampered and young.

Review: Avon Anew Genics Treatment Cream:

10 years in the making... Genics is revolutionizing anti-aging skin care ... says Avon...Building a customer base from scratch in a new location is difficult. I'm struggling with it this week, and I find myself behind in absolutely every area of my life. I know this is normal, expected, and utterly ordinary, especially with young boys and a cadre of animal companions. A better Avon rep would be more organized. A better rep would make more timely moves, not float through a dry-dock November by the seat of her kilt.

One of the products Avon is pushing on television is the fairly new Avon Anew Genics Treatment Cream, a face cream designed to "undo damage and turn back time." Even though I don't own or watch

Product Reviews

a television, I know all about the commercials thanks to my customers. None of them can remember the product's horrendously long name - neither can I! Everyone asks for the "brown tub" with the "gene science cream." More than one person has pointed out to me how insane the names of these new Avon Anew products are starting to sound. Just this one product name contains - not counting the "Avon" – NINE syllables!

Avon is spending precious brochure space promoting this Fountain of Youth Cream. (What? You think I'm gonna type out those nine syllables? You're nuts!) Many of the recent catalogues sport a two (or more!) page spread decorated in muted browns and creams with a cascade of DNA-like imagery. "Formulated for every woman, it's designed to reactivate your skin's own Youth Gene." Avon promises the goop will reverse wrinkles, restore contours, and repair damage. The advertising folks add some shocking percentages to add excitement and urgency to the literature. "100 percent showed more-even skin tone." One hundred percent?! Wow!

I tried this product last September during its huge roll out. It smelled fresh, rich, like the kind of expensive French facial cream you would try at Sephora and wish you could afford to purchase. The color is unusual - brown and almost metallic in hue, and the lotion smoothes easily into your skin. I promptly posted a mini review a few days later:

Look. I usually give nice big thoughtful reviews, after a good week or two or three or four of good-faith use of any new Avon product. I'm going to do this with the new Anew Ultimate Elixir Premium, too. But holy ordained cows on pogo sticks; I don't know how I'm going to get through a two-week trial! This stuff is giving me whopper zits!!!!!

Yeah, it was bad. I almost threw the stuff in the bin with a note to any dumpster divers to STAY AWAY! At forty-years-old I sported several constellations and a nebula or two across my cheeks and chin for a solid three weeks, my worst break-out since high school. But I continued to apply the product - figuring that perhaps my skin was undergoing a detoxifying bout - and as days turned into weeks turned into clear skin, turned into one month, than two, I started to actually see some small gains in skin health and texture.

Two months later the nine-syllable DNA cream (and THAT title is one syllables less than the real name!) remains a part of my daily regimen. My skin is softer and more even-toned than when I started using the Avon Anew Genics Treatment Cream (ah, just once more for laughs). No more November blah skin! This is not a miracle cream - I still have fine lines and wrinkles and some blotchy sectors along my hairline - but it is a nice addition to anyone's skin care routine. Just be warned that you may experience and uncomfortable transition as your skin adjusts to the product!

Review of Avon Anew Clinical Advanced Retexturizing Peel:

Most of my customers are interested in the Avon Anew Advanced Retexturizing Facial Peel. Avon promotes this product in television and print advertising. The company promotes it as an at-home alternative to a professional peel, and claims that it peels away dullness, dryness, and age damage so that healthier skin cells can surface, giving you a more youthful, creamy appearance. This product is not cheap. It costs $25.00 and is good for thirty applications.

I purchased the peel for myself during my first campaign. I wanted to be able to speak from experience when I tell customers what this product does, what it feels like, how it smells, and what results it truly produces over time. One month later, I'm ready to talk.

The facial peel comes in an elegant white tub. You feel like you purchased it at a dermatologist's office. You open the canister and inside are a stack of glycolic acid-soaked pads. They look exactly like those pads you used in high school to help get rid of pimples. You take a pad and wipe it all over your face, avoiding the delicate eye area. There are thirty pads in the container, stacked one on top of each other like Pringles. The advertising says that the pads have no scent, but if you sniff closely you can smell the acid, a mild acrid aroma.

The first day I tried this, I was alarmed at the tingling sensation. Holy cow! It felt like the skin was burning off of my face! I have never been so afraid trying a beauty product, and I include my one and only Brazilian bikini wax in this assessment!

After this process, my face was as red as a beet. I thought perhaps after a week or so I wouldn't have such a strong reaction, but I do, every time. Avon recommends that you use this product every other day, day or night.

Four weeks later my skin has improved. I would have to accurately say that the texture and clarity of my skin (excepting the whopper zit I had two days ago) has significantly improved. I also have more even skin tone and a healthy glow.

The Bottom Line: Excellent product, it DOES work. I will continue to use this product, so don't you dare try to take away my white container!

Review of Avon Anew Advanced Wrinkle Corrector:

The Avon Anew Advanced Wrinkle Corrector costs thirty-two dollars for a sleek white one-ounce container. Avon claims that it plumps lines and wrinkles from the inside out. The advertising is like the rest of the Clinical line of products - official, dermatological, serious, in shades of muted gray and cream.

Avon claims the Wrinkle Corrector smoothes fine lines and wrinkles overnight! The literature lists specific benefits: after one week, 82% of women felt their skin was rebuilt and renewed. With continued use 97% of women showed a visible reduction in lines and wrinkles. The numbers blink at you as you stare at the brochure, in white on dark gray paper, telling you they came straight from the white coat of a clinical study.

Now, I'm no spring chicken. I'll be the ripe age of 46 in a few days. I have small laugh lines, eye lines, and forehead lines. I never cared much about wrinkles. But after reading the advertising, I was excited to have them! It's the perfect opportunity to engage in a little clinical study of my own.

I opened my first container of Avon Anew Advanced Wrinkle Corrector two weeks ago. The bottle feels heavy, even though you can close your hand around it and hide it from prying eyes. When I twisted off the lid, I understood the heft of it. Most of the weight comes from the thick sides of the glass-like container. The product inside is vaguely off-white, not the peach color indicated in the print advertising. It smells light and fresh, with undertones of vanilla.

I decided to make my study as scientific as possible. My eyes had symmetrical sets of laugh lines. I would use the product on my right eye, only, and leave my left eye bereft of potential benefit. If, in two weeks, there was a drastic difference, then I would be convinced of Avon's claims.

The cream felt soft and cool. It has a viscous feel to it, like egg whites. It instantly seeps into your skin and leaves it feeling like velvet to the touch. I enjoyed applying it each evening before bed. After my first application, I rushed out of bed the next morning to see if my skin was, indeed, rebuilt and renewed. I couldn't believe it. My left eye looked worse than the right eye, albeit very slightly. So far so good.

Two weeks later, the results are in. I'm impressed. My right eye looks much younger than my left eye, and even my skin tone is improved and more elastic. Some of the fine lines have nearly erased, and the larger ones are more plump and youthful looking.

I highly recommend the Avon Anew Advanced Wrinkle Corrector and will continue using it! However, I am going to have to get my left eye up to the beautiful level of my right eye. Maybe I should apply the product morning and night to it until it matches its partner...

Product Reviews

I Animal Tested an Avon Product!

The night before last I woke up at two in the morning because my dog was whining and scratching at the wall. Now, my dog is known for her neuroses, but this was new and disturbing behavior. I sat up and stared, let my eyes adjust to dim light, but she continued to scratch and whine. And then I heard it. A strange loud gnawing sound coming from the wall behind my open door. A rat. A BIG rat, too, the way that sucker was scritching and scratching against my internal two-by-fours.

Tree rats are the scourge of my coastal town. They live in the tall palms, fat, content, nesting, and sneak down tree at night to forage the gardens and garbage of the rich and poor alike. Everyone's got 'em. I don't care if you live in a rock-lined castle on Skyline Drive or a small apartment in the barrio, you've got rats. Several companies work the rat problem in my area, setting traps in attics and returning once a week to retrieve rotting carcasses. And I thought Avon was difficult work.

I shushed my dog and shoved her outside. I didn't want to wake my boys. And I sat on the edge of the bed with my head in my hands, pondering my options. I could wait until morning to deal with the rat. I could dig through the garage and find the old rat traps I kept in a box for just such an emergency. I could call one of those Rat Emergency Men and report an infestation. And as I sat and thought and listened, the rat grew louder and louder, almost thumping against the wall. I knew I could not sleep. Images of the rat finding a way inside the body of the house and nipping at my sleeping toes washed into my vision and I stood up and declared war.

I searched through the garage in vain. I shone a dim flashlight into every box in my garage but no rat traps. Damn. And then I spied it - the pepper spray swinging from a plastic holder on my beach cruiser bike. I could stun the rat! And shove him in a box! I grabbed one of a hundred empty Avon boxes piled in stacks by the garage door and the pepper spray. I pushed down on the spray switch, testing the trigger, and Hssssssss. Nothing blew the space but stale air and one gray flake of desiccated pepper madness. Crap. I had to figure out a new option.

I tiptoed back through the house with my box and set it on the floor under the attic access outside my bedroom. The rat continued feasting and nesting, a hearty claw claw claw against wood-grain, then a running in circles pattern, rinse, repeat. I looked around my bedroom for a good weapon. Books, banjo, pillows, nothing seemed safe or rodent-worthy. I looked in the bathroom, too, for good measure, and grabbed the one item that might do the trick - my Avon Advanced Techniques Volumizing Mousse for Fine Hair. I opened the hatch and pulled down the miniature ladder and tossed the box in, following close behind.

The attic was dirty and dark. I held the mousse in front of me like a stun gun and crouched as quietly as I could, listening for my intruder. I heard him gnaw and arrange, gnaw and arrange, only twenty feet to my left and three feet down. I pushed the box across the floor of the attic and kept the mousse at hand. The gnawing stopped. I stood still, waited, held my breath. And then BAM! The rat scurried up a hole in the floor and toward me! I screamed! I squeezed the mousse trigger and an arc of heavy foam hit the air, flew, fell, right on top of Mr. Rat! I screamed again, watched the rat flail against the floor, rubbing one arm against his face to clear the sticky material. I slammed the box open side down right over his body and sat on the box, breathing heavy, listening to my boys jump from bed yelling Mom! Mom! Mom!

I called 17 to climb the stairs and sit on the rat box while I looked for a good piece of plywood to slip underneath, and we carefully carried the Rat of the Covenant out of the attic, out of the house, upside-down box on four feet of plywood. We carried it all the way through the night to my cranky neighbor's house three houses down the street and my boys ran for cover. I grabbed one point of the box, angling my feet to run for home, lifted the box and zoomed the h-e-double-toothpicks outta there. The rat ran for cover, hopefully my neighbor's bed, and I collected the box and board and walked home.

I'd have to be honest and say that the Avon mousse didn't do a thing for that rat's hair. But perhaps today he is re-groomed and gnawing on new furniture, sleek, shiny, and full of volumizing body.

11 Guerilla Marketing Avon Techniques!

Sometimes you just have to think outside the box!

1. Include a little post-it pad imprinted with your name and number and a pen with every Avon brochure. This will make it easy for your customers to remember to write down their orders and call you.

2. Around here, many business people use their vehicle license plates like a business card. I think more people have vanity plates than the regular state-issued plates! I think most states allow you to have seven letters or numbers on a vanity plate. How about registering AvonLdy in your state? Or AvonGrl, Avon4U, MyAvon.

3. When Avon discontinues an item or reformulates it, sometimes I am left with half a dozen tubes or so of the older version. It can be difficult to sell these. I have to deal with the hassle of returning items, so I came up with a great solution. I donate any of these older products to my church's rummage sale. I make sure to put a big sticker with my contact

info on the side of the items that says "Donated by Your Avon Lady, Birdie." If someone is buying Avon at a rummage sale, they probably use and enjoy Avon products on a regular basis. It's a great way to make some new customers and help your church or other organization out at the same time.

4. I started making a CD each campaign of the best deals in the brochures, plus a few customer testimonials for both me as an Avon Rep and for some of the new products. My customers love listening to the CD. Some of them slip it into their car deck on their commute to work. It has increased my sales by at least 30 percent.

5. Some customers call me with their order, and some of them send me emails. Often times a customer will forget to say which brochure she is ordering from. Sometimes she might forget her product number or the color of the makeup. I used to give customers the order form that Avon sends us for our customers but it is so small and the print is too tiny for some of my older customers. To help keep me organized I made a simple LARGER PRINT easy-to-follow order form for my customers. It has a clearly-marked space where customers fill in which brochure they are reading so I can match up product prices, and each line instructs the customer to fill in product number, color, size, and quantity. So much easier! I rarely have product mixups now.

6. I don't ever visit a customer unless I bring a snack to share with me. Even if I'm just dropping off an order or a brochure, I bring a little bag with homemade biscotti. It's a small gesture, but it really makes my customers see me as a real person. I bake biscotti once a week and wrap them in that nice colored plastic wrap, and tie it at the top with a pretty color-coordinated ribbon. A few biscottis can make a customer's day. Some of my customers are addicted to the goodies, and I even think they order sometimes just to get one of my double chocolate biscottis!

7. I made a one-page flier with my contact info and the latest Avon brochure specials, and then place one in every book and magazine related to beauty, in every library within driving distance.

8. Around here, some of the restaurants have those drawings for a fee

lunch. You have to drop your business card in a fishbowl or can, and one card a week is drawn. I drop my card in every restaurant's bowl, but I tape two samples on it so that it will get looked at, and on the back I write:

"I don't want the free lunch, I want to treat YOU instead!"

9. Sponsor an Easter Egg hunt in your yard and have eggs for the kids with treats inside, but have special eggs for the parents with special Avon goodies. You can stuff the eggs with special coupons and samples and small, inexpensive products like the Easter-themed lip balms. Choose a specific color for your Avon Eggs so that the moms know which eggs to find! Watch those women run!

10. I found that a winning combination is to place some food item in a little baggie and place that in the plastic bag with the brochure. A favorite in some of my neighborhoods, is a bagel. You should see the husbands wrestle the wives for the Avon brochure! I'd stay away from the onion bagels, but trust me, bagels work.

11. Take your brochures and go on a Saturday or a Sunday morning to barber shops and walk in and give them to the men to give to their wives or girlfriends. Tell the men "Let me give you a tip. Are you married or have a girlfriend?" and when they say "Yes," you say "Tell your wife or girlfriend you'll give her fifty dollars to buy anything in this brochure. They won't believe what a great guy you are!

~ ~ ~

Not-Quite-A-Prank-Call to the Avon Representative Hotline Part Two

I stood in the same spot as my initial call, seven hours later. The sun bounced off my left shoulder, cast a fractured shadow of tired Avon Lady and backpack against a cracked adobe wall. A steady stream of students passed me. They carried books, homework, the disappointed expression of a lost Indian summer afternoon. A chipper voice greeted my ear, and I mentally crossed my fingers and opened my mouth.

"Hi! I need to know if you can use the Avon Astonishing Length Mascara on a show terrier! Is it safe?"

My stomach clenched as I waited for the response.

"Hon, is this your terrier? Or a customers?"

I paused, not sure whether to relax my tight muscles. A brown grasshopper landed on my flip-flop and I shook it, watched him jump, land on top of the wall.

"It's a customers show dog. I honestly don't know anything about terriers. Is this product safe?"

"Well, hon. If you're talking show dogs, what I would recommend you use is the Beyond Color Lash Fortifying Mascara. We have several champions using this product. It prevents lash loss and breakage. What else is your customer using?"

I held the phone away from my ear and looked at it. I wanted to pinch myself, see if I dreamed up this Avon Hotline Lady with the show dog knowledge.

"Uh, I don't know. She only asked about the mascara. What would you recommend?"

"Well, hon. You must have her try the new Avon Footworks Pedi Peel. Have you tried it? It will soften and condition a dog's calloused paw pads like nothing else. And of course she's using Skin So Soft for the coat?"

I don't remember much else, only remember grabbing my wire notebook and writing down a furious litany of Best Products for Show Dogs. I flipped the phone shut just as my boys met me at the corner.

"So, Mom! What did you do today? Sell any Avon?"

My older son, 11, ran his hands through his thick hair as his younger brother, 9, bent to the sidewalk and picked up a piece of rose quartz. The sun splashed our image, three connected beings, three levels, against the adobe, casting the lone grasshopper into shadow.

"Well. I didn't sell much Avon, but I learned how to make a terrier terrific!"

My boys didn't ask, didn't seem to know there was a question. We held hands, walked away from the sun, east, toward the great plains, toward our simple home.

Every Day Prayer!

81. Place Avon brochures, samples, and your Avon business card in the vestibules or community rooms of your local churches, temples, synagogues, mosques, and other places of worship. Include a flier explaining that you can provide a wonderful Avon fund-raising opportunity. You can add this line to your literature:

"Your body is a temple. Show your respect with Avon."

Better than an Apple!

82. Whip out the Avon at your Parent Teacher meetings this school year. Add this tagline to your Avon brochure:

"When it comes to beauty, there's always more to learn!"

Host an Avon Workshop!

83. Set up a series of free workshops at your local Elks Lodge, nursing home, library, or community center. Offer to teach your neighbors how to make the most of their makeup application, how to be the most beautiful bride, how to use Skin So Soft to solve every household problem. Teach your community a valuable skill using Avon products! Make sure to bring plenty of samples and brochures. Neighborhood community centers are always looking for teachers to provide fun and current information. Help your local world become a little prettier and smarter!

Free workshops can get free press in the local newspaper and on local radio stations!

Get it Together!

Meetup

84. Want to meet women and men who like to discuss beauty, skin care, and the latest products? Start a group at Meetup.com, the social network for meeting likeminded others in real life! Schedule your first Meetup at a coffee shop, and bring lots of brochures % samples. Have fun sipping cappuccino and listening to your new friends' beauty ideas and troubles. You will make new sales, and more importantly, new friends!

Suggestion names for your Meetup group: Beauty and the Beast, Makeup Chat, or Skin Care for Dummies.

Make a STRIKE for Beauty!

85. Bowling Alleys - Leave your cards, brochures, and fliers in the shoe changing area as well as the women's bathroom. Even male bowlers enjoy Avon products - how about a flier telling the Mens Bowling League teams that they can get a group discount on anti-fungal foot cream or Silicon Glove hand cream? On your fliers:

"Don't let rough hands pin you down: Try Avon!"

Plan with Avon!

86. Visit every party planner in your city and drop off brochures with cute gift items, sample-sized fun products like seasonal lip balms, and jewelry items circled. Event planners often have to provide Thank You gifts to visiting dignitaries. Why not help them provide Avon?

"Time to Party! Look your best with Avon!"

Set sail on your Cruise with Avon!

87. Local Cruise Ship agents and Travel Agents often gift big customers with baskets filled with trial sized travel items. Drop by the ticketing office with a demonstration basket and a price sheet showing the different kinds of gifts you can provide for their clientele!

Sail the Seas with Avon!

Pay it forward with Avon!

88. Attending a fundraising raffle, silent auction, or other benefit for your favorite organization? Donate a basket of Avon! Tape your card with contact information to your donation. Don't forget to include a brochure and some samples! Try to match your donation to the theme of the event, or include colors and scents that match the season.

Give the gift of Beauty!

89. Local theater troops and school acting programs need your Avon! Stage makeup can wreak havoc on the skin. Offer skin care samples to sooth angry skin, and bring a demonstration bottle of Avon Moisture Effective Eye Makeup Remover Lotion. On your fliers:

"Try Avon Moisture Effective Eye Makeup Remover Lotion and look your best on stage and off!"

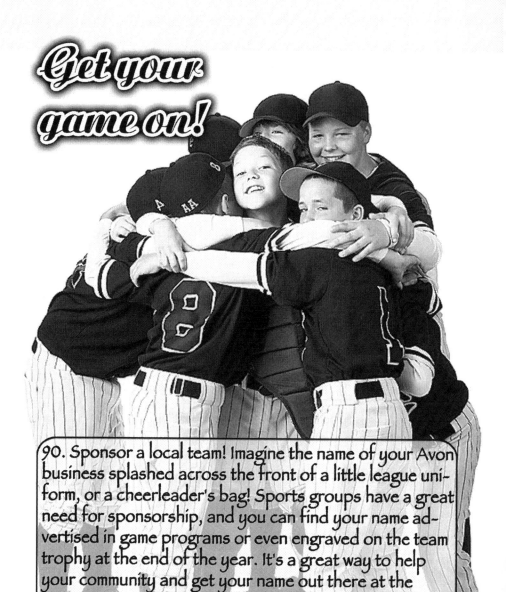

Get your game on!

90. Sponsor a local team! Imagine the name of your Avon business splashed across the front of a little league uniform, or a cheerleader's bag! Sports groups have a great need for sponsorship, and you can find your name advertised in game programs or even engraved on the team trophy at the end of the year. It's a great way to help your community and get your name out there at the same time.

Be a team player with Avon!

91. Courtrooms – many people spend hours waiting during trial – why not give them something to read and something to try? Courtroom workers appreciate Avon samples and brochures, too! Get a smile with:

"The jury is in on beauty – Avon wins!"

Avon – Your lifeline to beauty!

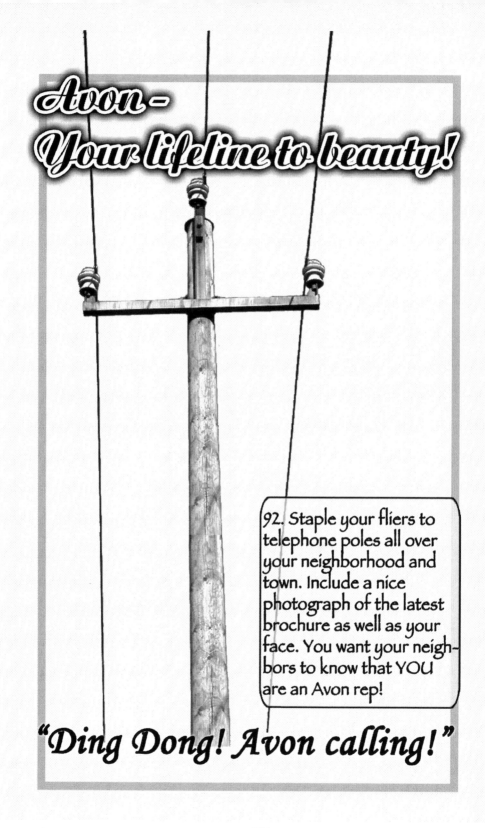

92. Staple your fliers to telephone poles all over your neighborhood and town. Include a nice photograph of the latest brochure as well as your face. You want your neighbors to know that YOU are an Avon rep!

"Ding Dong! Avon calling!"

Treat them Special!

93. Invite those who spend an average of $50 or more per campaign to join your free Preferred Customer Program. Offer these special clients a "behind the scenes" discount or buy-two-get-one free deal each campaign. Great customers should receive better-than-great service! Folks like to feel special, and offering your best customers a perk each new brochure will keep them coming back for more!.

Give them a laminated card with "Preferred Avon Customer" on it!

Let Avon be your personal shopping service!

94. Slip your brochures, fliers, and business cards next to products at the grocery your customer might purchase, such as skin care items and shampoos, near the baby care products like diapers and cans of formula. New moms, especially, don't have time to shop often. If they realize they can stay at home to purchase some of their needs, they will be thrilled!

"Stay at home mom? Stay at home to shop!"

Make Headlines!

95. Does your town have a local newspaper? Reporters, advertising layout designers, paper boys and girls, receptionists – everyone who works on the paper could be a great customer. Leave your brochures with some samples at the front desk. You can even ask the managing editor if you could pay a small fee and slip a business card or flier into each paper prior to delivery. Don't forget the "Penny Pincher" types of rags and the alternative weekly. A great tagline to add to your flier:

"Erase your "Headlines" with Avon Anew Line and Wrinkle Corrector!"

Start your journey with Avon!

96. Toll-booth attendants are stuck in that little box all day long! Why not surprise them on your next drive-through with an Avon brochure and some samples? Make them smile with:

"The road to lookin' great starts with Avon!"

Beauty Jocks!

97. You can find several locations at the gym to drop sales literature. The locker room is a great place to leave Avon samples – especially skin care products. Add these words to your brochure or flier:

"After the workout, it's time to play. Tone up with Avon!"

Construct your future with Avon!

98. If you have young children, hand out Avon brochures and samples to the moms and dads at the playground. Parents enjoy having an Avon brochure to peruse while their children play in the sandbox. Post a flier at the playground entrance that says:

"Don't play with your beauty routine - use Avon!"

99. Does your city have an airport shuttle service? Ask if you can furnish brochures for the vehicles. If the shuttle has to travel a ways to reach the airport, your potential customers will thank you for providing some entertainment during the ride.

"From airport to hotel to business meeting - let Avon take the helm"

Thank you.

100. Hospice. I often bring samples and trial sized products and donate them to the hospice. I never ask for a sale here, but have had grateful family members call me to order more products. This is a great time to simply thank those moving into another life.

A simple "Thank You" is all you need to say.

Know Your Product

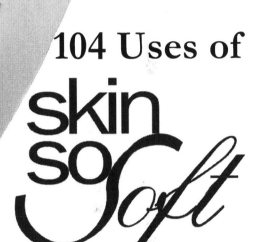

104 Uses of skin so Soft

1. It's a bath oil and after shower moisturizer
2. It can be used to remove makeup.
3. Great tanning oil (no sunscreen).
4. Hot oil treatment to soften cuticles.
5. Great massage oil for tired muscles.
6. Cleans off tape marks left from bandages on skin.
7. Cleans ink off the skin.
8. Insect repellent.
9. Helps relieve itching caused by dry skin.
10. Cleans oil and grease off of skin.
11. Painting something? Use Skin-So-Soft to remove paint from the hands. (Instead of turpentine).
12. It soothes light sunburn.

13. Rub hands with it before washing, it helps get them cleaner.
14. Rub on dry, cracked skin….helps heal skin in 2-3 days.
15. Put 1-2 caps full in liquid soap and use it for shaving legs and under arms. Helps razor glide and leaves skin feeling smooth.
16. Pour a little into your Foot Saver to help moisturize your feet while you relax them.
17. It removes chewing gum from hair, skin, and most non-pourus surfaces.
18. Cleans permanent ink off stamps.
19. SSS Original Bath Oil works GREAT on Head Lice. Saturate head and let it set for 15 minutes. Then rinse under an outdoor faucet. Shampoo hair a couple of times to get the oil out, but the lice should be gone and stay gone!
20. It kills ants instantly.
21. Spray on skin to relieve dry itching skin. Helps skin retain its elasticity.
22. Wash hair with shampoo and conditioner like always and after it dries… Use about the size of a dime of SSS and rub it in your hair. It goes straight in and leaves hair as shiny as the ads on TV, not greasy at all, just soft and shiny.
23. Use bath oil towelettes — cover window sill with towelettes to keep ants out.
24. Sometimes, using bath oil, like Avon's Skin So Soft, will work to loosen the glue which holds the nits to the hair. There is a product called Neon Nits, which when sprayed on the hair, will highlight the nits so you can see them to then snip them out with a small scissors.
25. Psoriasis on elbows. Try Avon's Skin-So-Soft bath oil spray on affected areas.
26. Bath use, fill bath with water and a little skin so soft, very relaxing and gets rid of dry skin.
27. Sponge it around doors, windows, and on screens to keep crawling bugs out.
28. It's a good wood cleaner and conditioner for natural wood.
29. It removes glue and gum left from price tags and labels from glass, metals, and most plastics.
30. It removes soap scum from shower doors and curtains, and bathroom and kitchen figures.
31. It removes lime and hard water deposits from fixtures, tile, shower

doors and windows.

32. It's an oil lubricant for fitting pipe joints that won't slip together.
33. It cleans ink off most vinyl and painted surfaces.
34. It cleans heavy oil and grease from non-porous surfaces.
35. It takes fur off off clothing.
36. Rub on brass ornaments or figurines to help keep them from turning dark.
37. Removes crayon from appliances and most painted surfaces.
38. Wash cupboards with it mixed in your cleaning water to keep ants off and out of the cupboards.
39. Use it to discourage hornets from building their nests. After using a hornet killing spray, remove the nest and keep the area sprayed with SSS. They will not rebuild there.
40. Use it to clean leather, it will also keep it soft and supple.
41. Use it on your air conditioning screen (filter)–your incoming air will smell fresher and the filter is easier to clean.
42. Rub all over window sills to keep ants out
43. It cleans paint brushes easily and leaves them soft as new.
44. It removes gum from carpets.
45. It removes scuff marks from patent leather shoes.
46. Use it on running rails for sliding glass doors and windows.
47. It removes "ring around the collar".
48. It removes liquid nail (paneling glue).
49. Two glass bowls or glasses stuck together? Drizzle a little S.S.S down the sides and they'll come apart easily.
50. It removes candle wax from furniture, carpets and clothing.
51. Hummingbird Feeders: To deter bees try rubbing SSS on the feeder surface by the feeder ports.
52. Maggots too!! You squirt SSS in can and lid, then later flushed with soapy water, you shouldn't have any bugs in cans rest of summer!!!
53. It is a great furniture polish!
54. Put it in one of those bottles that you attach to your backyard hose and then spray down the back yard! Will cut down on ants, mosquitoes and other creepy crawlies.

55. Spray it on rose bushes to keep the deer from eating them, (used at the cemeteries on the flowers for the same reason).
56. Kills spiders.
57. It cuts grease and cleans dirt from range hoods.
58. Add a capful to wash water of clothes…acts as a fabric softener and keeps the bugs off clothes.
59. Spray on orchids and other flowers for moisture and to keep bugs away.
60. Cleans baseball caps. Just spray on and rub with toothbrush.
61. Tomato Plants. Mix one part SSS and 2 parts water and spray on tomato plants to kept tomato worms off. Adding vinegar works fine too. Spray plants about every 2 or 3 days.
62. SSS bath oil also does a great job cleaning cherry wood cabinets.
63. Put a little in your mopping water to help keep crawling bugs out. (Not too much or the floor gets slippery.)
64. Use to clean windows.
65. Removes crayon from most surfaces.
66. It's a great insect repellent (or you can use Bug Guard, the actual SSS repellent)
67. Screens can be lightly sprayed with Avon "Skin-So-Soft" to repel no-see-'ums and tiny gnats that otherwise might slip though the screens.
68. Another use for SSS is it will kill those pesky earwigs. Spray it on & they don't return to life.
69. Also if you ever make candles, use clear wax and melt, put skin so soft in it and harden - works great for outside in the summer.
70. As a deodorizer, spray into air and let settle, kills those nasty pet orders.
71. Kids rooms if a child wets the bed, spray the bedding and sheets before washing and will give it a fresh clean smell.
72. It's a great insect repellent for your pet. (as recommended in "Outdoor Life" and "Field and Stream")
73. Mix 5 parts water, 1 part SSS and mist on animals. Brushing it in makes their coats gleam and keeps insects off (Great for Show animals).
74. Mix in your pet's bath water to remove fleas and in between spray

them with the same mixture as above to help keep them at bay.

75. Rub on your hands before and after working with your pets and farm animals. It will remove the strong smells.

76. Black Fly Spray For Dogs: Use as a spray or a dip. 1 cup SSS, 1/2 cup liquid detergent and 3 gallons of water.

77. For dog's dry skin mix 1 tablespoon of SSS per gallon of water and use as an after bath rinse. Or spritz your pet's coat once per week.

78. If your dog should get tar or asphalt on the pads of their feet rub on SSS and then wipe off.

79. Flea Bath: Use a flea and tick shampoo. Rinse so no soap residue is left. Follow with final rinse of 2 gallons of water mixed with flea dip and 1 capful of SSS. The SSS helps replace the oils lost in bathing and has the added benefit of repelling insects.

80. Flea Repellent: Avon's Skin So Soft Bath Oil. 1-1/2 ounces per gallon of water; used as a sponge-on dip (or as a spritz) has been tested and proven to have significant, but not complete, flea-repellent activity for a 6-day period.

81. It should help those dry coats, too.

82. Chow Dogs. Many chows have very dry and flaky skin. The SSS can help dandruff and itchiness and make hair shiny and smooth. It also serves as a great flea and tick protector.

83. Another Insect Repellent Recipe for Pets: 1 cup Avon Skin So Soft bath oil 1 cup white vinegar 1 cup (or more) water 5 cc of essential oil of citronella (from the health food store NOT the type you burn to keep insects away that is available in a drug store) Mix in a spray bottle. Straight SSS works well for mosquitoes too but really makes your dog greasy.

84. Barns. Use of an inexpensive fly control spray or a diluted mix of Avon Skin-So-Soft in water can be sprayed on barn walls and floor to discourage insects from hanging around or to eliminate them before putting in the new bedding. As time permits, and if you can keep your goats out of the barn for a few hours – let the barn stand and air out before re-filling with bedding.

85. Rub on your hands before and after working with pets and farm animals, takes away pet odor.

86. A natural way to help cats with flea problems and flea allergies is to rub Skin So Soft into the skin. Fleas don't like it!

87. Cats: SSS IS SAFE FOR FUR LICKING ——-The SSS plus is safe as long as it is the one without sunscreen.

88. Pet's with Sensitive Skin: Don't overuse the SSS. Just use the lotion, and rub it into the skin, not more than every few days.

89. SSS can be used as a hoof polish. Put's a nice shine to the hoof without drying it. The farrier's wife will appreciate this one!

90. SSS can be used on pet accessories such as collars to shine them up.

91. Horses with dry skin: Bathe like normal and then I put a capful of SSS in a 5 gallon bucket of warm water and sponge this all over. Their hair coat dries silky soft and stops itching.

92. The bug guard towellettes we had last summer work great on the horse's ears and around their eyes.

93. When banding (braiding) their manes use the Techniques Oil Sheen. It seems to help hold the braids a lot better and they don't try to rub them out.

94. The dry end serum works great in their tails as a detangler. The products are a heck of a lot cheaper than actual horse products.

95. It removes tar spots from the car without damage to the paint.

96. Use it to clean vinyl dashboards, seats, and tops. It not only cleans, but keeps the vinyl soft and helps to prevent any cracking.

97. After washing your car, use it as a tire dressing to keep them looking like new.

98. Put some on a small washcloth and leave in the car to help keep the air fresh and clean.

99. Wipe down vinyl surfaces inside your car. Cleans nicely and removes smoke odors left by cigarette smokers.

100. It gently cleans heavy grease and oil from skin and non-porous surfaces (great for Mechanic's Hands).

101. It removes tree sap.

102. Prior to traveling...rub SSS on headlights and grill. It makes insects and bugs easier to remove.

103. Shines vehicle tires

104. Open a towlette and use as an automotive air freshener.

These *104 Uses of Skin So Soft* are just one of the many downloads available on my website, 100WaysToSellAvon.com. Print them out and include them with all of your Skin So Soft deliveries - increase your sales and your reputation with your customers!

About the Author

Birdie Jaworski lives and writes in New Mexico.

Birdie's memoir of her time selling women's cosmetics door-to-door, "Don't Shoot! I'm Just the Avon Lady!" was nominated for a Pushcart Award.

Birdie's collection of real-life short stories set in rural New Mexico, "My Tiny Vegas," includes stories about the secret Scientology mesa outside of Las Vegas, New Mexico, as well as heartwarming stories about green chile, santeros, and life on the edge of the Great Plains.

You can visit Birdie's website at birdiejaworski.com.

More Books from Birdie!

<u>My Tiny Vegas</u>: Birdie Jaworski lives on the edge of the eastern plains of New Mexico, where the Sangre de Christo Mountains meet the Great Plains, smack in the middle of the town of Las Vegas. No - not the big City of Sin with the gambling strip! Las Vegas, New Mexico is not as well known as other Wild West towns, such as Dodge City, Deadwood, or Tombstone, but she is said to have been the worst of the rowdiest Old West towns. She's still rowdy, still mysterious, still full of larger-than-life characters! Doc Holliday kept his medical office in Las Vegas, New Mexico. The Rough Riders held their first reunion in the saloon of the Plaza Hotel in Las Vegas. You can get a shot of tequila in that same saloon, today. Let Birdie share her beautiful tiny Las Vegas with you..

<u>GALLINAS</u>: For generations everyone and everything from Native Americans, barbed wire fences, Hispanic settlers, hot springs, Jewish traders, piñon trees, railroad moguls, ladybugs, the virgin of Guadalupe, adobe bricks, United States Calvary, acequias, Charles Lindbergh, the internet, Teddy Roosevelt, the Catholic church, Hollywood directors, annual monsoons, Curanderas, longhorn cattle and itinerant saints have left their mark on the inner and outer landscapes of Northeastern New Mexico. This book excerpts the best and brightest pages directly from GALLINAS Magazine's sixteen month run, complete with local ads, 3am typos, and all the heart and soul of the original publication.

• And look for <u>100 Ways to Recuruit Avon Representatives</u>, due out early in 2012, with tons of tips and fun stories to give you information and motivation to help you take your Avon business to the next level!

Made in the USA
Middletown, DE
28 August 2017